formatio

TRADITION. EXPERIENCE. TRANSFORMATION.

Formatio books from InterVarsity Press follow the rich tradition of the church in the journey of spiritual formation. These books are not merely about being informed, but about being transformed by Christ and conformed to his image. Formatio stands in InterVarsity Press's evangelical publishing tradition by integrating God's Word with spiritual practice and by prompting readers to move from inward change to outward witness. InterVarsity Press uses the chambered nautilus for Formatio, a symbol of spiritual formation because of its continual spiral journey outward as it moves from its center. We believe that each of us is made with a deep desire to be in God's presence. Formatio books help us to fulfill our deepest desires and to become our true selves in light of God's grace.

SURRENDER

TO

LOVE

Discovering the Heart of
Christian Spirituality

DAVID G. BENNER

IVP Books
An imprint of InterVarsity Press
Downers Grove, Illinois

InterVarsity Press
P.O. Box 1400, Downers Grove, IL 60515-1426
World Wide Web: www.ivpress.com
E-mail: email@ivpress.com

InterVarsity Press ® *is the book-publishing division of InterVarsity Christian Fellowship/USA* ®, *a student movement active on campus at hundreds of universities, colleges and schools of nursing in the United States of America, and a member movement of the International Fellowship of Evangelical Students. For information about local and regional activities, write Public Relations Dept., InterVarsity Christian Fellowship/USA, 6400 Schroeder Rd., P.O. Box 7895, Madison, WI 53707-7895, or visit the IVCF website at <www.intervarsity.org>.*

Scripture quotations, unless otherwise noted, are taken from the Jerusalem Bible *(JB), copyright* ©*1966 by Darton, Longman & Todd, Ltd., and Doubleday & Company, Inc. All rights reserved.*

While all of the stories and examples in this book are based on real people and events, some names and identifying details have been altered to protect the privacy of the individuals involved.

Cover design: Cindy Kiple
Cover image: Victoria & Albert Museum, London, U.K./Bridgeman Art Library
ISBN 978-0-8308-2302-4
Printed in the United States of America ∞

Library of Congress Cataloging-in-Publication Data

Benner, David G.
    Surrender to love: discovering the heart of Christian spirituality
    /
    David G. Benner.
        p. cm.
    Includes bibliographical references.
    ISBN 0-8308-2302-6 (pbk.: alk. paper)
    1. God—Worship and love. 2. Submissiveness—Religious
aspects—Christianity. I. Title.
    BV4817.B356 2003
    231'.6—dc21

                                                                    2003001546

P	24	23	22	21	20	19	18	17	16	15
Y	23	22	21	20	19	18	17	16	15	14

To Juliet

CONTENTS

Preface

SURRENDER, LOVE
AND SPIRITUALITY

A few years ago I received an e-mail from a woman who told me she had greatly enjoyed my previous books but was furious over something she had discovered in a recent one. "I can't believe that you recommend surrender," she said. "As a psychologist, you of all people should know how dangerous it is to submit to someone." She went on to accuse me of being irresponsible as a spiritual guide and "a typical male" in my "uncritical acceptance of the way power is abused in relationships." I had obviously hit a nerve!

I will tell more of this woman's story in the pages that follow. It is a story that dramatically illustrates the transforming possibilities of surrender to divine love. But it also reminds us how frightening even the idea of surrender is to some people.

The concept of surrender has come upon hard times in recent years. Some view it as too close to submission; others associate it with codependence or an abdication of personal power. Consequently, the notion of surrendering to anything or anyone has become suspect.

However, despite the unpopularity of the notion, surrender plays a crucial role in the spiritual journey as understood by most major religions and spiritual traditions. Far from being a sign of weakness, only surrender to something or someone bigger than us is sufficiently strong to free us from the prison of our egocentricity. Only surrender is powerful enough to overcome our isolation and alienation.

Christians often focus on obedience more than surrender. But while the two concepts are closely related, they differ in important ways. As we shall see, surrender is foundational to Christian spirituality and is the soil out of which obedience should grow. Christ does not simply want our compliance. He wants our heart. He wants our love and he offers us his. He invites us to surrender to his love.

Christianity puts surrender to love right at the core of the spiritual journey. Christ-following is saying yes to God's affirming *yes!* to us. If it is anything less than a response to love, Christ-following is not fully Christian.

Christianity is the world's great love religion. The Christian God comes to us as love, in love, for love. The Christian God woos us with love and works our transformation through love.

In spite of the trivializing influence of romantic and sentimental views of love in Western culture, love is the strongest force in the universe. Gravity may hold planets in orbit and nuclear force may hold the atom together, but only love has the power to transform persons.

Only love can soften a hard heart. Only love can renew trust after it has been shattered. Only love can inspire acts of genuine self-sacrifice. Only love can free us from the tyrannizing effects of fear.

There is nothing more important in life than learning to love and be loved. Jesus elevated love as the goal of spiritual transformation. Psychoanalysts consider it the capstone of psychological growth. Giving and receiving love is at the heart of being human. It is our raison d'être.

This book is about love—not the soft, sentimental kind but the strong, spirit-transforming kind. It is about the paradoxical ways we often fear love and the way love uniquely offers release from our deepest fears. It is about the consequences of building the spiritual journey around anything else than surrender to love. And it is about knowing ourselves to be deeply loved by God as the first step in becoming genuinely great lovers of others and God.

But because this book is about love, it is also about surrender and spirituality. Love invites surrender, and surrender is at the core of spirituality. The interweaving of love, surrender and spirituality flows out of both the nature of love and the nature of human beings.

Carl Jung suggests that love and spirituality share many connections and surrender is the most important of them. Love "demands unconditional trust and expects absolute surrender. Just as nobody but the believer who surrenders himself wholly to God can partake of divine grace, so love reveals its highest mysteries and its wonder only to those who are capable of unqualified devotion."[1]

Surrender is as much a part of genuine love as it is a part of authentic spirituality. Love invites abandon and intimacy. Love speaks to the depths of our soul, where we yearn for release from our isolation and long for the belonging that will assure us we are at last home. Love speaks the language of the soul as it awakens our hunger for relationship and connection.

The deepest ache of the soul is the spiritual longing for connection and belonging. No one was created for isolation. "Nothing in creation is ever totally at home in itself," says John O'Donohue. "No thing is ultimately at one with itself."[2]

We seek bridges from our isolation through people, possessions and accomplishment. But none of these are ever quite capable of satisfying the restlessness of the human heart. To be human is to have been designed for intimate relationship with the Divine. This is why the yearning for connection is spiritual. Our needs for love, connection and surrender form the spiritual core of our personhood.

For most people, nothing awakens feelings of deep terror like the experience of absolute disconnection from others. But in the same way, nothing vitalizes the human spirit like the experience of a loving connection—something that assures us that we are not alone and that we count for something to someone.

Love is the glue of connection. Love is the source of the deepest wellsprings of human vitality. Love is the only hope for overcoming our isolation. Love invites surrender and offers the intimacy and deep connection for which we long.

In my work as a psychologist and a spiritual director I am blessed to be able to accompany people as they learn to give and receive love. Journeying with others toward psychospiritual wholeness has been a rich opportunity for me to learn about love. Much of what I will present in what follows comes from these experiences.

But my personal journey as a human being and as a Christian has been even more important in this learning. Here I discover how easy it is to know that I am deeply and unconditionally loved and yet continue to strive to earn love. Here I learn how much I resist the very love that holds the promise of freeing me from my striving and fears. Here I learn how profoundly hard it is to make genuine progress in the school of love. And here I learn the most about how surrender to Perfect Love holds the promise of wholeness and holiness.

Those on the Christian spiritual journey form my primary audience for what follows. My own journey is being worked out as a Christ-follower, and my understanding of love is grounded in my experience of being loved by the Christian God.

However, while love plays a distinctive place in Christianity, the experience of love is obviously not restricted to Christians. The ability to love others is the pinnacle of fulfillment and health for all persons. Receiving the gift of love reminds us all of what it is to be fully human. What follows, therefore, should be of interest not just to Christians but also to those pursuing other spiritual paths, as well as those not consciously on a spiritual journey of any sort.

Surrender, love and spirituality—the big themes of this book— are, I believe, the big themes of life. In spite of the messages of Western culture, personal fulfillment lies in connection, not autonomy. Spirituality is the discovery of the fundamental connection that exists between us and God—a connection that then properly aligns us to others, the world and our deepest self. Love is the welcome that tells us that this is where we truly belong, the assurance that we have at last found our place.

All Saints' Day
Tao Fong Shan Christian Centre
Hong Kong

I

IT ALL BEGINS
WITH LOVE

Take a moment and try a simple exercise. The results will tell you a great deal about the nature of your spiritual journey.

Imagine God thinking about you. What do you assume God feels when you come to mind?

When I ask people to do this, a surprising number of people say that the first thing they assume God feels is disappointment. Others assume that God feels anger. In both cases, these people are convinced that it is their sin that first catches God's attention. I think they are wrong—and I think the consequences of such a view of God are enormous.

Recently I talked with the family of a fourteen-year-old boy referred to me by his mother, who had caught him dressing in her clothes. His parents were shocked and disgusted by this behavior, and they told him that God was equally revolted. When they discov-

ered that he had been cross-dressing for some time—occasionally
with another boy his age—they said that unless he immediately and
permanently stopped he was no longer welcome in their family. They
also assured him that God would damn him to an eternity in hell.

It was not much of a surprise to discover that this boy's view of
God was pretty similar to that of his parents. He told me he knew
how disgusting he was to God. He said he had stopped asking for
forgiveness, as he couldn't control what he thought and did. Coming to God was simply too painful. He was convinced he knew how
God felt about him, and it was not welcoming.

This makes me think about my own family. My parents expressed
their love with a reserve that reflected their British background and
Canadian culture in the 1950s and 1960s. It was clear, however, that
they loved my brother and me deeply. And it was clear that nothing
either of us could do or not do would ever change that fact. I know
that at times I disappointed my parents. All children do. But this was
never their preoccupation. With certainty I know that when they
thought of me they felt deep and unqualified love. This made it easy
for me to believe them when they told me the same was true of God.

Regardless of what you have come to believe about God based
on your life experience, the truth is that when God thinks of you,
love swells in his heart and a smile comes to his face. God bursts
with love for humans. He is far from being emotionally unin-
volved with his creation. God's bias toward us is strong, persistent
and positive. The Christian God chooses to be known as Love, and
that love pervades every aspect of God's relationship with us.

BUT . . .

After saying this, however, I think I hear a "but" that bursts forth
from some readers. As I have encountered it when speaking on

this topic, it often takes the form of "But you are forgetting about sin. Sin changes everything, especially how God feels about us." I disagree. I am neither forgetting sin nor minimizing its significance. I will have more to say about sin shortly, and I think it will be clear that I take it seriously. But I do not think that sin changes everything, particularly how God feels about humans. God is simply not that fickle. Like loving parents who can look at their children with disappointment that in no way dilutes their love, the God in whose image such parents are made loves us with a love that is not dependent on our behavior. If at least some humans can do this, how dare we question God's ability to do the same?

God's love is never compromised by anger. The presence of anger does not mean the absence of love—particularly in God. Love is God's character, not simply an emotion. What a small god we would have if divine character was dependent on our behavior. The Christian God is not like this. The Christian God is slow to anger and rich in mercy (see Exodus 34:6, echoed in Joel 2:13 and many other places in Scripture). He is quite unlike the god we would create if we were making him in our image.

I said that the answer to this question about how God sees us has important implications for our spiritual journey. Think for a moment about how Christ-following develops if you assume God looks at you with disgust, disappointment, frustration or anger.

The central feature of any spiritual response to such a God will be an effort to earn his approval. Far from daring to relax in his presence, you will be vigilant to perform as well as you possibly can. The motive for any obedience you might offer will be fear rather than love, and there will be little genuine surrender. Surrender involves relaxing, and you must feel safe before you can relax. How could anyone ever expect to feel safe enough to relax in the presence of a

God who is preoccupied with their shortcomings and failures?

I have known many Christians like this. The parents I described at the beginning of this chapter thought of the Christian life as measuring up to divine expectations by avoiding sin. This leaves little room for grace, little room for knowing and enjoying God or resting in his love. The boy's father assured me that as a Christian I should understand that God and sin simply cannot go together. It was not my place to debate theology. But I knew that while he wanted to uphold the holiness of God, he had absolutely failed to understand Christ's incarnation. The Christian God doesn't turn away from sinners in disgust but moves toward us, bringing us his redemptive presence.

Perhaps not surprisingly, Christians who assume that God is preoccupied with sin tend themselves to adopt the same focus. In fact they often seem to think that they honor God by taking sin as seriously as they do. Sometimes they judge other Christians by how seriously they seem to treat sin. Often they become uncomfortable with an emphasis on divine love; they feel an urgent need to balance this by highlighting God's hatred of sin. Unfortunately, while they may give intellectual assent to God's love, they often experience very little of it.

What a different relationship begins to develop when you realize that God is head-over-heels in love with you. God is simply giddy about you. He just can't help loving you. And he loves you deeply, recklessly and extravagantly—just as you are. God knows you are a sinner, but your sins do not surprise him. Nor do they reduce in the slightest his love for you.

Perhaps you find yourself wanting to believe that this is true of God but still not convinced. Fortunately, we do not have to be uncertain about God's attitude toward us. It is clearly revealed in the life and teaching of Jesus.

THE PRODIGAL FATHER

Jesus' parable of the prodigal son illustrates God's love wonderfully. The subheads in our English Bibles, however, title this parable wrongly. The story is about the character of the father, not the misdeeds of the son. The focus is on the prodigality of the father— a man extravagantly lavish with his love. This classic story (Luke 15:11-32) remains my favorite story in all of Scripture.

Once upon a time a rich man had two sons. One day the youngest son became impatient waiting for his father to die and asked for his share of the inheritance. With sadness the father agreed and gave half of all he had to the son, who took it and left immediately for a distant country. There he squandered everything and, faced with destitution, took a job feeding pigs.

One day as he sat with the pigs, he thought of home. It suddenly struck him that his father's servants lived much better than he. So he returned to his father, ready to ask his forgiveness and offer to work as a servant. Seeing him coming, his father was filled with joy. He ran to meet his son, gave him his own ring and robe, and ordered that the fattest calf be killed for a welcome-home celebration.

Hearing this, the older brother was furious. In all the years his irresponsible brother was away, he had faithfully fulfilled his responsibilities and had never asked for anything beyond what he deserved. But a party like this had never been thrown for him! Filled with righteous indignation, he refused to join the fun.

Now it was the father's turn to come to him. "My faithful son," he said with love, "you have always been with me, and everything I have is yours. But we must celebrate the return of your brother, because he was dead and has now come back to life; he was lost and is now found. This calls for a party!"

Every time I read this story it warms my heart and settles me in

God. It reminds me that far from focusing on my sins, God sees me through eyes of love. All my fears about how God will respond to me in my sin wash away as I see the Father running to meet me. Why did I stay away so long? How could I have ever thought he would let me come back as a slave? Clearly I never need to fear returning to him—no matter what I have done or not done—because God's love has nothing to do with my behavior.

But while I can identify with the younger son, I feel an even stronger connection with his older brother. I identify with his dutiful, plodding obedience. And I identify with his self-righteous resentment of the Father's generosity. How he longs to relax in the Father's love.

The story ends at a poignant moment. We do not know if the older son will be able to relinquish his effort to earn love and accept the father's invitation to take his place at the feast.

Part of me—and I suspect part of all of us—wants to earn the Father's love. In the story *both* sons fall into this trap, and both have to learn the same lesson. The Father's love reflects the Father's character, not the children's behavior. My behavior—whether responsible or irresponsible—is beside the point. Responsible behavior does not increase the Father's love, nor does irresponsible behavior decrease it.

How much we need to believe this. Our Christ-following would be quite different if we did.

CREATION AS A LOVE STORY

But the centrality of love to Christianity does not begin with Jesus and his teaching. Love has its origins in the character of the triune God, where perfect love is shared within a sacred community of three. And love, by its very nature, always reaches out. Rather than be content with the circle of love within the Godhead, God reached out to create so that others could enter this sphere of intimacy and be warmed by divine love.

The creation story is seriously misunderstood when it is read as science. Instead it should be understood as a love poem. Pay attention to the imagery of the creation account and see if it doesn't carry striking overtones of love. It begins with the Spirit's hovering over the unformed elements of creation (Genesis 1:2). The image is of a bird protecting and nurturing new life that is forming under her.

Last spring during morning prayer walks by a lake near our home, I often watched a pair of white swans. I watched them select a location for their nest and then take two weeks to carefully construct it. Day after day the male brought reeds to the female in his beak. She took these from him and chewed them until they were soft enough to form into the nest. Carefully she then wove them together, shaping the container for the new life that was about to emerge from within her. As soon as she finished the nest, the female swan settled on top of it; she did not move for several more weeks. Even through days of heavy rain and unusually cold weather, she sat there without stirring, except to reach out and eat the food brought to her in the beak of her partner.

Suddenly one day I saw beneath her what I had been watching for—a little ball of fluffy white down. Still the mother did not move. She continued to sit on her young chicks, only gradually allowing them to begin to creep out from underneath her. Then in perfect rhythm with the young chicks' first moves toward independence, the mother's attentive and protective presence began to allow space for growth—all the while never letting the chicks out of her sight and continuing to hover over them.

This is the image of the Spirit of God that is presented in the

Genesis story. Even in a shapeless state, the universe receives maternal gentleness and devoted attention from God. The Spirit hovering over the unformed earth is a picture of God's tenderness and loving presence. It is an important part of the creation love story.

But then, as the world comes into being, the Creator God pronounces each successive act of creation "good." God is obviously thrilled with his work. Far from the indifference or hostility that an artist might feel toward a disappointing work of art, God delights in what he creates. His affirmation of goodness is not simply an evaluative statement. It is love bursting forth in an expression of joy and pleasure.

God's love is the source and fulfillment of all creation. From the beginning God's love has been evoking life in all its abundance. It is "the passion—the oxygen, the flame, the glue—fueling, firing, connecting the universe in its amazing array."[1] Apart from the ever-creative outflow of God's love there would be nothing but darkness, void and nonbeing.

God's love is the source of everything that is, and this is supremely true of human beings. God becomes even more directly involved in the generative processes as he fashions humans in his image. Even more remarkable, now he shapes his creations with his hands and vitalizes them with his breath. His delight in seeing the result is like the joy of a parent on first seeing a newborn child. He expresses his pleasure by declaring humans to be not just good but "very good" (Genesis 1:31). Effusing with exuberance, God's love spills forth into creation, and the result is women and men.

Creation is an outpouring of love—an overflow of love from the heavens to earth. Creation not only declares the inventiveness and resourcefulness of God but reveals the abundance of his love.

Creation declares that humans are born of love and for love, created in the image of a God who is love. Love is our source and love is to be our fulfillment.

Made in God's image, humans are invested with a nonnegotiable dignity. We are compatriots of God, not just creatures of God. Even more astounding, God chooses us to be his friends. That imputed status was never annulled, despite our sinful rebellion and declarations of independence.

Creation was God's plan for friendship. We were not brought into existence simply so that we could worship God. Nor were we created simply for service. Human beings exist because of God's desire for companionship. We are the fruit of God's love reaching out toward creatures who share enough similarity that relationship is possible.

Humans were created for this intimate communion with their head-over-heels-in-love Creator God. When God thinks of us he feels a deep, persistent longing—not simply for our wholeness but, more basically, for our friendship. This possibility lies at the core of our own deepest desires. It also lies at the core of our deepest fulfillment.

THINGS GO TRAGICALLY WRONG

So far it sounds like a perfect story. If this Christian understanding of the nature of God is accurate, one might wonder how things ever turned out so badly. How did we end up where we are?

Created from love and for love, humans—according to the Christian account of things—spurned God's love in favor of what was perceived to be freedom. The result, of course, was disastrous. Liberty was instantly replaced by bondage, intimacy by alienation. Genuine love was reduced to self-love, and the result was egocentricity and estrangement from our deepest self, God and others.

All of us live with love despoiled. It appears to be the best we can experience and the best we can give. The love we receive from others is always limited by their brokenness and finitude. And the love we give to others is always contaminated by our self-preoccupation. We long for perfect love but easily become discouraged about the possibility of ever deeply experiencing it. And so we content ourselves with a pale imitation of the love for which we were intended.

This is certainly my own story. The love I have received from my family, wife and friends has been more wonderful than I could ever deserve. But the love I have passed on to others has often been stingy and inconsistent. I know God's love more deeply than I did even a few years ago, yet I still find myself sometimes hiding when I hear him calling to me in my inner garden. Why do I remain afraid of love though I have never been seriously hurt by it? Why does it continue to be difficult for me to surrender to Perfect Love? My story points me back to my own sin and dysfunction. For things are clearly not as they should be.

Deep down, however, something within us seems to remember the Garden within which we once existed. Part of us longs to return; we know that this is where we belong. But another part of us seems bent on living out our illusions of freedom and autonomy. We tell ourselves that we can create other gardens in which to find soul rest and encounter love. But what we create are weed-infested gardens of compulsion and idolatry. Instead of rest we get addiction and self-preoccupation. And our restlessness grows, our hearts yearning for something both familiar and unattainable.

Faint residues of a memory of Perfect Love seem to flit at the edges of human consciousness. Such memories are so weak that they are easily ignored. They remain, however, the core of our deepest desires—all human longings pointing to the Source.

AND NOW FOR THE GOOD NEWS

Fortunately, the story does not end here. God's identification with his creation through the incarnation is the second installment of the Great Love Story. Realizing that we had forgotten our story, God sent Jesus as the personification of love. The Son came to reveal the character of the Father. The Son came to bring us back to the Father—back to love.

Jesus came to remind us what true love really is. Christians and non-Christians alike widely affirm the nobility of Jesus' character. He was so obviously a good man. His love was obvious, his teachings were noble.

But his life, death and resurrection all point us beyond this. They point us toward the character of God. This was what Jesus himself taught. With truly remarkable boldness he asserted that his life revealed God. The love he demonstrated was the love that was his source. It was the love he knew from eternity as the Son of the prodigious Father.

Who else, then, to better remind us of our own story? Who else to better bring the faint residual memories of the garden of love in from the periphery of consciousness to the core of our being? The story of Jesus is the story of love personified. We miss the point when we simply try to do what he tells us to do. And we miss the point when we merely try to follow the pattern of his life. His life points us back to his own Source. His life is intelligible only when it is understood as the personification of divine love.

But genuinely encountering Love is not the same as inviting Jesus into your heart, joining or attending a church, or doing what

Jesus commands. It is the *experience* of love that is transformational.
You simply cannot bask in divine love and not be affected.

Angie[2]—the woman mentioned in the preface who reacted to
my use of the term *surrender*—illustrates what can happen when
God's love is actually experienced. Angie had good reason to fear
surrender. She had been emotionally abused by her parents, raped
by a boyfriend at college and then raped again by the chaplain she
approached for help. She had been taught that God was love, but
she had no personal experience of this. Trusting God or anyone
else was difficult. But her hunger for God—which was God's
greatest and most surprising gift to her—would not allow her to
reject him.

Angie's encounter with God's love came through meditation on
the Gospels and a supportive relationship of spiritual direction.
What she discovered was that the God she thought she knew was
actually quite different from the God who is revealed in Jesus. She
was astounded by Jesus' care for women. Nothing had prepared
her to encounter a God who could be as countercultural as Jesus
was in that regard. She was also surprised and impressed by the
fact that he always seemed to take the side of the disenfranchised.
She had always felt like an outsider, and God and religious people
had always seemed like insiders. Suddenly she saw Jesus in a different light. Now he was on the outside with her. She was also
deeply moved by the tenderness and trust of Jesus' relationship to
the Father. Somehow this made God safer. If Jesus could trust
God, perhaps she could also.

Slowly Angie's heart of pain, anger and mistrust was softened.
Gradually she lowered her defenses and dared to receive God's
love. And slowly but surely she was transformed by love.

Jesus came to lead us back to Love. He came to play the central role in the world's greatest love story. But it was not, of course, simply an enactment. He was the Son of Love who came to show us the love that is our destiny, our healing and our fulfillment. He came to reveal the Perfect Love for which we long and to which we belong. And he came to show us what surrender to such love would look like.

KNOWING GOD, KNOWING LOVE

Ask Christians what they believe about God, and most will have a good deal to say. However, ask the same people what they know about God from direct personal experience, and most will have much less to say.

Many will speak of knowing that their sins have been forgiven. Some will speak of answers to prayer or a sense of God's presence. But many will fall strangely silent. Many—even evangelicals who talk the most about a personal relationship with God—will not have much to say about how they actually experience God in that relationship.

A. W. Tozer notes that most of us who call ourselves Christians do so on the basis of belief more than experience. We have, he argues, "substituted theological ideas for an arresting encounter; we are full of religious notions but our great weakness is that for our hearts there is no one there."[3]

Any authentic spiritual journey must grow from direct, personal experience of God. There is no substitute for a genuine encounter with Perfect Love. "Knowledge by acquaintance," Tozer affirms, "is always better than mere knowledge by description."[4] Knowing God is not simply a matter of believing certain things about him. Personal knowing goes beyond objective knowing.

Think for a moment about knowing your spouse or best

friend. If this is a genuinely intimate relationship, you would never confuse knowing this person with holding correct views about her or him. Genuine knowing—personal knowing—involves much more than head knowledge. It involves a relationship; it involves the heart.

If God is love, he cannot be truly known apart from love. He cannot, therefore, be known objectively. One cannot observe him from a distance and know him. To do so is to fail to genuinely encounter his love. One can encounter divine love only up close and personally.

Looking back, I find it remarkable how easily I accepted ideas about God as substitutes for direct experience of him. It took me a long time to begin to know God through my heart and not simply my head. In my depths I longed to really know the God toward whom my heart was drawn. But all I seemed to be able to find was beliefs. I believed that God was love, and if I thought about it, I could see that this meant he loved me. But I didn't know that love on a deep, persistent personal basis. God's love was an idea, not a personal experience.

In later chapters I will say more about how this began to shift for me. But let me be clear at this point that it is possible to know God's love *personally,* beyond simply knowing *about it.* The fact that I am deeply loved by God is increasingly the core of my identity, what I know about myself with most confidence. Such a conviction is, I am convinced, the foundation of any significant Christian spiritual growth.

On being asked if he believed in God, Carl Jung reportedly answered, "I don't believe in God, I know God." If this sounds presumptuous, recall Jesus' own words about the matter. Praying to his Father God, he said, "Eternal life is this: to know you, the only true God, and Jesus Christ whom you have sent" (John 17:3). The knowing that counts is personal and experiential. It is never simply impersonal, objective knowledge about God.

This is the major theme of the first epistle of John. John argues that "love comes from God, and everyone who loves is begotten by God and knows God. Anyone who fails to love can never have known God, because God is love" (1 John 4:7-8). These are bold words. But they seem pretty clear.

Describing my wife to someone who has not met her, I often say, "To know her is to love her." She is just that sort of a person. But how much more true this is of God. To know the Christian God is to experience love. One cannot genuinely encounter the Christian God and not encounter love—first as love received and subsequently as love returned.

St. John of the Cross, one of the great mystics of the Christian church, said that God refuses to be known except by love. Christian mystics are not as different from the rest of us as we may think. They are simply people who emphasize direct personal experience of God and are reluctant to accept any substitute for this. As thinking creatures we cannot help forming thoughts about our experience. But if our experience of God is limited to our thoughts about him, we have not genuinely encountered God. And if we confuse our thoughts about God with personal knowing of God, we confuse theology with spiritual experience.

Tozer—perhaps the most widely known and respected of evangelical mystics—testifies of the possibility of experiencing a continuous and unembarrassed interchange of love with God. He goes on to speak of "this intercourse between God and the soul" as being capable of being known "in conscious personal awareness . . . as any other fact of experience."[5] It is not something that requires deduction from either theology or the Bible. God's love can, he asserts, be known "as certainly as we know material things through our five senses."[6] It can be the reality on which we build our life.

But listen to another, even better known, Christian mystic on this. Talking about young Christians for whom he had spiritual responsibility, he prayed that they might be so grounded in the love of Jesus that is beyond knowledge that they would be "filled with the utter fullness of God." Who was this bold person who dared to equate experiential knowing of the love of God with being filled with the fullness of God? None other than Paul the apostle of Jesus, his words recorded in Ephesians 3:14-19 and his life demonstrating the conversion that occurs when one encounters Love.

IS THIS FOR YOU?

It may be that you are growing uncomfortable with my emphasis on a love relationship with God. Perhaps you judge yourself to be more rational than emotional and conclude that the relationship with God I am describing is for someone else. But is love really a need of only some of us?

The deepest need for all human beings is to surrender to Perfect Love. That need—and love itself—will, however, be experienced differently by different people.

The problem with thinking in terms of personality types is that people too easily put themselves (or others!) into a box and fail to encounter the parts of self that don't fit into that box. No matter how good the system of personality classification, the best typology captures only a small part of the uniqueness of persons. Large parts always remain outside the box. And the parts that are outside the box (parts that Carl Jung called the shadow) need development if we are to become truly whole.

Encountering God in love is as important for people who live in their head as for those who live in their heart. Both need to learn to ground their identity on experiential knowing of themselves as deeply loved by God. But each will face different challenges in doing this.

Tending to not know or trust feelings, people who live predominantly in thoughts and rational analysis need to learn to embrace their feelings. Doing so is a way of becoming more fully alive and fully human. Such people—and I count myself among them—have forgotten how to experience the world through feelings. Feelings bring new data that is missing when only thoughts are trusted. Genuinely meeting God in love, not simply in thoughts, will therefore always be deeply growth-producing.

People who live in close contact with their emotions need to learn to move beyond the superficial feelings that are the center of their experience to a deeper and more genuine emotional encounter with the world. Such people do not need fewer emotions; they need deeper and more truly authentic ones—the ones from which they defend themselves with sentimentality and superficial emotional responses. They also need to learn to embrace critical thinking, by which feelings can be judged and reality more firmly embraced. Genuinely meeting God in love offers an opportunity to move beyond sentimentalism and emotionalism. It offers a chance to truly encounter love, to critically reflect on the meaning of that love and to ground oneself in it.

All of us long for a deep personal encounter with Perfect Love.

And all of us need to have our identity grounded in being deeply loved by our divine Lover. Sentimentalism, emotionalism, rationality and analysis all sabotage the development of such a relationship. Talking about such a relationship is easy. Actually coming to develop a love relationship with the invisible God is far from simple. It doesn't happen automatically for anyone.

Subsequent chapters will examine in more detail exactly how it does happen. But first we must reflect on why we so often fear that for which we most deeply long. We turn in the next chapter, therefore, to a strange bedfellow that is never far from love—fear. For until we understand the complex interaction of these two opposing dynamics of life, we will not be fully prepared to encounter love with the surrender for which we long.

FOR FURTHER REFLECTION

Does it seem hard to believe that when God thinks of you, love swells in his heart and a smile comes to his face?

If your identity does not rest on knowing yourself deeply loved by a God who is head-over-heels in love with you, spend some time prayerfully meditating on several passages. First, however, let me describe what I mean by meditation.

Christian meditation is like spiritual daydreaming. Rather than analyzing or thinking about the passage, simply let yourself soak in it. There is no need to do anything with the words you read. Instead let them do something to you. Don't be preoccupied with examining what is happening. Just allow the words to turn over in your mind and wash over your heart.

Prayerfully reflect on the following biblical passages one at a time, taking as much time for each as you wish. Transformation demands more than a momentary experience of love. It demands sufficient basking in this love that being deeply loved becomes the foundation of your identity.

- ☙ Psalm 23
- ☙ Psalm 91
- ☙ Psalm 131
- ☙ Isaiah 43:1-4
- ☙ Isaiah 49:14-16
- ☙ Hosea 11:1-4
- ☙ Matthew 10:29-31
- ☙ Romans 8:31-39

2

LOVE AND FEAR

Einstein stated that one of the most important questions facing every individual is whether or not the universe is friendly. It would appear that for the majority of human history most people have not believed that it is. The gods seem to be either indifferent or hostile to humans. In either case they seem to require appeasement—something to get their attention and earn their favor.

Religion based on appeasing the gods is not restricted to less developed countries and non-Western cultures. If you look at how people actually relate to their god, it becomes apparent that large numbers of people live in a universe they consider to be unfriendly. Even among Christians, the love they believe to characterize God often does not seem to translate well from theory into practice. Their God is still a God who requires appeasement—gestures and beliefs to earn favor and escape wrath.

My own spiritual journey began with frantic steps to ensure that I escaped God's punishment. After several years of hellfire sermons,

I did what any reasonable ten-year-old child would do under the circumstances—I accepted Christ into my heart and began seeking to live a life that would please God. My motive for doing so was predominantly punishment avoidance. I was told that salvation was a gift of love, but it seemed strange to ask me to accept a gift at gunpoint. I tried to believe that God was a God of love, but what was prominent in my mind was his justice and holiness. I saw little that invited surrender. My obedience was out of duty, not devotion, and my earliest steps on the spiritual journey involved covering my bases to minimize risk; they were not steps of surrender to love.

Thank God my story didn't end there. The hunger God had planted in me for him left me longing for a relationship with him, not simply a way to avoid hell. Slowly a shift in my experience of God began to take place as I learned to meet him in my emotions and senses, not just my thoughts. This process was helped by the prayer practice I recommended at the end of the last chapter. Slowly but steadily, fear of a God whose wrath was primary began to be replaced with surrender to a God whose love was primary. It made all the difference in the world for me.

Love and fear stand in a complex relationship to each other. Ever since Eden, the human struggle has been "to escape from the grip of the spirit of fear and to be open to the embrace of love."[1] The words of John that perfect love casts out fear (1 John 4:18) communicate an absolutely profound psychospiritual truth. But how are we to understand the fact that so many people who bask in love continue to slither in fear? Surely this suggests that love is overrated as a transformational power. How else could we explain why we sometimes seem to love our fear and fear the loss that would be involved in giving fear up?

Christianity seems to give mixed messages about fear. On the one hand, the Bible repeatedly tells us not to fear. In fact, "Fear not" is one of the most common greetings of an angel or our Lord himself to humans. It seems God understands that fear is a natural response to a god. Telling us to set aside our fear should therefore comfort us, reassuring us that God is not as we expect. But on the other hand, we are also repeatedly told to fear God (Deuteronomy 10:12; 1 Peter 2:17). We are also told that the fear of God is the beginning of wisdom (Proverbs 1:7) and the most appropriate response to one who can kill not only the body but also the soul (Matthew 10:28). So should we be afraid of God or not? Is fear the enemy, or is it a spiritual virtue?

Some Christians bristle at the notion that love, not fear, should characterize their response to God. It overturns everything they have learned about how to position themselves in relation to the cosmos and the divine. In a strange way they have actually become comfortable with an unfriendly God who should be feared. Not settling for awe or reverence, they live with a fear of the God who keeps them in their place by ensuring their continued distress.

Is this the response that the Christian God invites from us? I am convinced it is not. The Christian God wants the intimacy of our friendship, not our fear. The Christian God comes to us with gestures of breathtaking love, hoping to eliminate our fear, not manipulate us through it. And he offers his love as the one thing in the universe capable of making an otherwise hostile cosmos into a friendly home. He offers his love as the one thing in the universe capable of freeing us from our fears.

FACES OF FEAR

One of the things that block us from gaining freedom from fear is that most fearful people don't think of themselves as afraid. Unless their fears are focused on something external (such as snakes, heights or crowds), most people in bondage to fear fail to recognize the true nature of their inner distress.

Phaedra, a young woman who contacted me after reading one of my books, would have never described herself as fearful. But when we got together to chat about her spiritual journey, it was quite apparent that fear was a massive impediment to her surrender to divine love.

What first struck me about Phaedra was how apologetic she was about taking my time. Though I assured her she was taking nothing that I was not freely giving, she told me several times how busy she knew I must be and how concerned she was not to take advantage of my willingness to meet with her. I also noticed how careful she was to craft her statements in a way that would avoid misunderstanding. When I commented on this, encouraging her to relax and simply tell me her story, she replied that carefulness in speech and life was deeply ingrained. I sensed that she spoke the truth.

Phaedra lived her life within narrow boundaries and in measured doses. *Caution* and *control* were her watchwords. They were comfortable parts of the only self she knew. They were also masks of fear—fear of being misunderstood, fear of making a misstep and fear of being out of control.

Beneath her well-controlled exterior I sensed enormous passion and energy. But she feared her longings and held them in careful check lest they disrupt her equilibrium. It was, however, becoming increasingly hard for her to ignore her spiritual restlessness. Her spirit was responding to God's Spirit, and she was being wooed to relinquish control and surrender to the divine Lover of her soul. It was this deep longing that brought her to me. More important, it was this deep longing that gradually drew her into a love relationship with God.

Fear that has not found a way to attach to external sources is very hard to identify. It has many faces, all of which mask its essential nature. Some people fear intimacy while others fear solitude. Some fear loss of control while others fear a loss of image. Some fear the strength of their feelings while others fear the loss of some comforting feeling. Some fear attention while others fear neglect. Some fear life while others fear death. Some fear pleasure while others fear pain. Some fear loss of love, while others fear love itself.

But fear can be even more elusive than this. Sometimes it can have no face at all. If it is successfully avoided, it leaves almost no trace of its presence. And so those of us who are good at avoiding our sources of fear may come to conclude that fear has no part in our story. But we are mistaken. Fear—though not experienced—is still present and a source of bondage.

It took me a long time to become aware of the presence of fear in my life. I had virtually eliminated fear by investing enormous amounts of energy in avoiding failure and criticism. I didn't think of myself as fearful, because I was generally successful in avoiding what I feared. But doing so required compulsive over-achievement. It also required that I stay on the treadmill of earning respect by surpassing any reasonable expectations anyone could have of me. Obviously I was paying a very high price for my avoidance.

I found my fears when I experienced a significant personal failure in my mid-forties. Suddenly I was confronted with the ghost I had run from all my life. Its name was failure. It was shocking to discover how much I feared it. But it was also liberating. Acknowledging my fear has helped me to meet God in my places of deep vulnerability. And it has helped me meet others with greater honesty and humility.

Fear works in such a way that the object of the fear is almost irrelevant. Fearful people are more alike than the differences between the foci of their fear might suggest. Fear takes on its own life.

Fearful people live within restrictive boundaries. They may appear quite cautious and conservative. Or they may narrow the horizons of their life by avoidance and compulsion. They also tend to be highly vigilant, ever guarding against life's moving out of the bounds within which they feel most comfortable.

Because of this, fear breeds control. People who live in fear feel compelled to remain in control. They attempt to control themselves and they attempt to control their world. Often despite their best intentions, this spills over into efforts to control others. Life beyond control is unimaginable, even though their efforts at control have only very limited success.

Fear also blocks responsiveness to others. The fearful person may appear deeply loving, but fear always interferes with the impulse toward love. Energy invested in maintaining safety and comfort always depletes energy available for love of others.

DYNAMICS OF FEAR

This interaction between fear and love was noted by the Danish philosopher and theologian Søren Kierkegaard.[2] Kierkegaard devoted much of his life to the study of fear. He also spent most of his life struggling with it. Even though his insights did not provide him much personal help, they were profound.

Kierkegaard makes three invaluable contributions to our understanding of fear. He suggests that (1) fear occurs when the human spirit is afraid of itself, (2) fear is often a substitute for guilt, and (3) guilt always results in an inhibition of love.

These insights were discerned only in embryonic form by Kierkegaard. A more complete understanding did not come until the rise of psychoanalytic psychology after his death. Kierkegaard was on the right track, however, and well ahead of his time in understanding the nature of fear.

The notion of being afraid of one's self points to the inner conflict that lies at the core of fear. Although the object of one's fears may seem to be external, the real source of the fear is internal. The danger is within. The enemy is one's own self—or at least some aspects of the self.

Often the part of self that is most disturbing for people plagued with fear is their emotions. Typically they fear the strength of their feelings, particularly those feelings associated with impulses to action. Anger, sexuality, and any of the inner urges and desires all feel disruptive because they are all capable of leading to action. Consequently, people may attempt to shut down all feelings and thereby eliminate the urges that lie behind them. But this only compounds the sense of danger, because now they also fear a lapse of control.

This was clearly the case for Phaedra. What she most feared was the strength of her feelings. She worried that if she allowed herself to really feel anything strongly she might have to act on it. And she intuitively knew that doing so would force her to abandon the self-control behind which she hid.

One particularly important feeling that often lies at the root of fear is guilt. The part of self that is dangerous in this situation is the self that is felt, in some nonspecific way, to have failed or done something dreadfully bad. These feelings are not usually conscious. But they tend to seep into consciousness as fear.

Graham told me that fear had been a lurking companion for many years. He had been sexually abused by an uncle as a child and had trouble feeling safe in relationships with men since then. But he also felt somewhat inadequate and uncomfortable with women, and over time this led to a generalized fear of all social interaction. Most people had no idea that he experienced so much fear, as he took great pains to not give in to it. But he knew it was destroying his life.

Graham's sense of guilt was rooted in his experience of having been sexually abused. Although it was not rational, he had a vague feeling of being responsible for what had happened. His fears helped him defend against these deep-seated feelings of guilt. By avoiding people, he managed to distance himself from his inner torment. Fear was the price he unconsciously chose to pay to eliminate the guilt.

When this happens, the displaced guilt tends to be betrayed by compulsions. Compulsive niceness might, for example, reflect a neurotic sense of guilt associated with not being nice enough—perhaps being too aggressive or selfish. Or compulsive busyness might arise from guilt associated with feelings of being lazy. The problem is not real, objective guilt. The root of the fear lies in unrealistic expectations of the self—expectations, for example, of always being loving or always being productive. Such expectations lead to increased efforts to perform and inevitably result in performance failures. This then only serves to reinforce the neurotic feelings of guilt.

If these feelings are faced directly, their unrealistic nature is quickly identified and their effects dissipated. If, however, the guilt is repressed, it is easily transformed into fear.

Graham's compulsions centered on avoidance of anything that had the potential of reminding him of his sense of guilt. Although his fears were painful, his avoidance of intimacy with people protected him from something even more painful—the sense of being a person who was so dangerously powerful that he could cause others to behave irresponsibly and abusively.

But as noted by Kierkegaard, unresolved guilt always damages the capacity for love. The reason for this is that the guilty self feels that it deserves punishment. It also feels like a dangerous self. Unconscious guilt makes me feel that I have to withdraw from others lest I damage them by my love. This leads to self-preoccupation, and the result is always a serious impairment of my ability to give or receive love.

In Graham's case, the disturbance of his ability to love was dramatic. Although he longed for intimacy and surrender, he feared the ways he might poison any love relationship. Love itself had become dangerous because unconsciously he perceived himself to be dangerous.

But let us return to the words of John. For in a single verse (1 John 4:18) he summarizes these insights, anticipating by a millennium and a half the best psychological understanding of fear developed in the last two hundred years: "In love there can be no fear, but fear is driven out by perfect love: because to fear is to expect punishment, and anyone who is afraid is still imperfect in love." I know of no more succinct summary of the dynamics of fear.

These words also point to love as the antidote to fear. A later chapter will take up this truth. For now, however, we need to further explore the way love itself sometimes becomes the object of our fear.

FEAR OF LOVE

Graham is not alone in his fear of love. Millions of people fear intimate relationships because they have experienced rejection or abandonment by a parent, friend or lover. They avoid getting close to people because they fear they will be hurt again. Such a reaction is tragic, even if quite understandable.

Love is dangerous precisely because it invites surrender. Although we may try to give and receive love in measured doses, both our own deepest longings and the very nature of love bid abandon.

But abandon brings us right up to the edge of an inner abyss. We are suddenly confronted by a series of "what if" questions, all of them pregnant with potential peril. What if I surrender to this love and am again hurt? What if I abandon myself to this lover and he or she fails me? What if I reveal myself and am rejected? What if I am overwhelmed by the strength of my own need for love? Or what if I am overwhelmed by the devouring nature of the love of the other?

Adult love inevitably reconnects us to the earliest experience of infantile dependence on our parents or caretakers. And no parent is perfect, and no one's earliest experiences of love are consistently and absolutely positive. These and later disappointments in love sometimes surface when we are faced with love as adults. As a result, some people find themselves unable to let go; they seem to prefer the familiarity of their fears to the potential danger of the unknown.

Some caution at the point of abandon is always appropriate. Crippling anxiety that makes commitment to love impossible is, however, always sad. And saddest of all is when this anxiety stops us from encountering Perfect Love—the one thing that has the potential to heal us of our fears.

PERFECT LOVE

The Christian God is unlike any god humans could ever imagine. In fact, the Christian God operates in a manner so often unlike what we even want or are ready to receive that it is obvious that such a God is no mere projection of human imagination or desire. The great distinctive of the love of the Christian God is that there are no strings attached to it. God simply loves humans. He created us for a love relationship with himself, and nothing that we can do—or not do—changes the love he bears us.

The notion of God's loving us unconditionally is absolutely radical. As Philip Yancey has written, "The Buddhist eight-fold path, the Hindu doctrine of *karma,* the Jewish covenant, and Muslim code of law—each of these offers a way to earn approval. Only Christianity dares to make God's love unconditional."[3] The God Christians worship loves sinners, redeems failures, delights in second chances and fresh starts, and never tires of pursuing lost sheep, waiting for prodigal children, or rescuing those damaged by life and left on the sides of its paths.

The Christian God of grace stands in stark contrast to the vindictive, whimsical, threatening and often capricious gods of other religions. Only the Lord God unconditionally cherishes human beings. Only the Lord God forgives all our offenses and teaches us how to forgive ourselves. Only the Lord God provides everything he demands. Only the Lord God offers the life of his own Son for the salvation of his people. The Lord God's persistent habit of relating to humans with grace is the best news the human race has ever received.

The good news of Christianity is something that we would have never discovered if Jesus had not come and shown us the character of God. Everything within us tells us that the universe must be organized according to a principle wherein we get what we deserve. But quite unbelievably, God is not simply the projection of our own image on the cosmos; he is different from anything we could have ever imagined. He offers us something we could never deserve—forgiveness of our sins and his embrace of love.

What makes grace amazing is that it and it alone can free us from our fears and make us truly whole and free. Surrender to God's love offers us the possibility of freedom from guilt, freedom from effort to earn God's approval, and freedom to genuinely love God and others as the Father loves us.

"THANKS, BUT NO THANKS"

While one might expect humans to receive the news that God is unequivocally for us as good news, in reality we do not. We have such an inborn tendency to run our own life and to pay our own way that unconditional love is both unbelievable and terrifying. In short, we want nothing of it.

Grace is totally alien to human psychology. We want to get our house in order and *then* let God love and accept us. The psychology of works-righteousness and self-certification is foundational to the human psyche and totally at odds with grace.

The deep-seated way humans resist divine grace helps us understand something about the fear of love. While some people fear any love, what most of us resist is unconditional love—perfect love. The reason for this is that such love demands surrender.

A familiar Christian hymn states that as I come to God, "nothing in my hands I bring, simply to thy cross I cling." How deeply I resent this fact. How desperately I want to be able to contribute something to the deal—my faith, my effort, my love, my belief. But the bottom line is that Perfect Love meets me where I am and asks only that I open my heart and receive the love for which I long.

It is surrender to love that I really resist. I am willing to accept measured doses of love as long as it doesn't upset the basic framework of my world. That framework is built on the assumption that people get what they deserve. That's what I really want. I want to earn what I get. And for the most part I am content to get what I earn. Nothing grates more than a handout. If you doubt this, just ask someone who lives off charity. What humans want is to earn the love we seek.

The Christian God comes to us as wholly other—so different from the gods of my imagination, so far beyond my control. Encountering such a God is terrifying because encountering perfect love is an invitation to abandon ego. A god of our own making would be much less terrifying. But such a god could not offer me what I most deeply need—release from my fears and healing of my brokenness.

LOVE OVERCOMES FEAR

The Christian God understands all this. He has a big advantage. He created us and knows us intimately. He knows how we respond to anything that threatens our need for control. And he knows how we fear the abandonment that perfect love invites.

This is the reason God's first words to us are "Fear not." This is not a command but an invitation. God understands our tendency to fear. And in gentleness he invites us to let him rid us of our fears and heal us by love.

The story of Moses and the burning bush illustrates this well. According to Exodus 3:1-12, one day while tending his sheep, Moses noticed a bush that was on fire. Approaching it, he saw something strange. In spite of the fact that it was burning, it was not consumed. Now his curiosity was really piqued. He began to go closer. Suddenly an angel called out a warning—"Moses, Moses! . . . Come no nearer." Curiosity instantly turned to fear.

Confusing fear and reverence, some Christians think God wants us to feel afraid of him. They might assume that the angel's call to Moses was designed to teach him the fear of the Lord. But

I would suggest that it was designed to protect Moses from danger—the danger of a presumptuous approach to the divine that failed to recognize God's holiness. God didn't want Moses to stay away. Indeed he wanted Moses to approach him, because he wanted to share his heart with him. But he wanted Moses to approach him as the Holy Other.

What God next told Moses was that he was aware of the suffering of his people and longed to deliver them. He showed Moses his face, and it was a face of compassion. Quite unlike a god who wants people to fear him, Yahweh wanted Moses to know that he is a God of tenderness who suffers with those who suffer and longs for their release from all that binds them.

Discovering that God was a God of compassion, Moses began to feel less afraid. Fear instantly returned, however, when God told him his plans for the rescue. He was to go to Egypt and bring the captives back with him. Moses was overwhelmed with his inadequacy and the magnitude of the job. "Who, me? How could I ever do that?"

God's answer was the point of the whole encounter, the reason he had called Moses aside and shared his heart with him: "I shall be with you" (Exodus 3:12).

God does not want us to stand back in fear. What he desires is reverential intimacy. He wants us close enough to him that we know his heart—close enough to hear his heartbeat. He wants to look into our eyes, and he wants us to look into his.

The story of Jesus walking on the water toward Peter and the other disciples in the boat illustrates this same point (Matthew 14:22-33). First, notice that Jesus invites Peter to come to him on the water. Jesus invites intimacy, invites surrender. In faith Peter stepped out of the boat, and to his amazement, he didn't sink! But when he began to look at the waves rather than Jesus, instantly he began to be submerged. Fear suddenly replaced amazement, and he cried out with panic, "Lord, save me!" And "Jesus put out his hand at once and held him."

Perfect Love overcomes fear.

Jesus is the antidote to fear. His love—not our believing certain things about him or trying to do as he commands—is what holds the promise of releasing us from the bondage of our inner conflicts, guilt and terror. Jesus comes to us to show us what God is like. Knowing how we would react to a god who suddenly turned up on the human scene, God becomes human, to meet us where we are and minimize our fears. The incarnation is God reaching out across the chasm caused by our sin and starting the relationship all over again. The incarnation reveals true Love reaching out to dispel fear.

Fear would have kept Angie—the woman whose story I have been telling—from trusting God, had she not slowly become convinced of God's deep love for her. First she had to learn that it was all right for her to bring her fears to God. That was the only way she could come. Her fears were with her continually until she came before the face of Perfect Love. As she soaked in God's love—daring to believe that this was the fundamental truth of her identity—slowly she watched her fears drop away. And she was surprised to discover that she was beginning to feel love for God. It was not something she tried to produce. It simply happened. Her heart had been touched by God's heart.

FOR FURTHER REFLECTION

If this chapter drew your attention to some of your own fears, take some time to reflect on them. Don't draw back from them. Face them in the full light of day, naming them for what they are. It is

the things in ourselves that we refuse to face that have the greatest
potential to tyrannize us. To deny the reality of fears is not to
know ourselves, and then we risk becoming possessed by that
which we refuse to face.

But if it were easy to face our fears, we would have already done
so. So something must be different to allow you to really face
things you previously avoided. That difference is love.

The courage to face unpleasant aspects of our inner self comes
from feeling deeply loved. It also comes from the assurance that we
are safe. Our gaze needs to go back and forth between divine love
and our fears. We gain courage to face our fears as we soak in love.

Meditation on aspects of Jesus' life and teaching can help you
further ground yourself in perfect love. Let the following brief
scenes lead you into meditative daydreaming. Picture yourself in
each situation. Observe, listen and note all the sensory elements of
each scene. Notice your feelings. And pay close attention to Jesus.
Allow the experience to begin to teach you about being deeply
loved. And as you do so, begin to face the fears that have held you
back from surrender to this love.

>   *Matthew 19:13-15*. Join Jesus as people bring little children to
    him to be blessed. Hear the disciples as they scold the par-
    ents, telling them not to bother the Master. Then hear the
    words of Jesus: "Let the little children alone and do not
    stop them coming to me; for it is to such that the kingdom
    of heaven belongs." Picture yourself coming to Jesus as one
    of those little children. Crawl up on his knee and feel his
    touch as he lays his hands on you and blesses you.

>   *Matthew 22:1-14*. Read these words about the invitation to a
    wedding feast as if they were an invitation to you to bring
    all the lame, broken and fearful parts of yourself into the

banquet of love being prepared for you by the God of perfect love. Dare to bring these neglected parts with you. There is a space reserved for each, and each is welcome in the circle of God's love. Allow these neglected parts of yourself to enjoy the warmth of God's love as they are honored with special treatment.

- *Mark 6:45-52.* Join the disciples in the boat as they face a mounting storm. Notice Jesus walking on the water toward you. Hear his words of comfort: "Courage! It is I. Do not be afraid." Then observe as he gets in the boat with you and the others, and as the wind—and your fears—suddenly decreases.

- *Luke 12:22-32.* Listen to these words of Jesus as if they were spoken for the first time directly to you. Pay close attention to what Jesus says about how valuable you are to him. Hear his love for you, and notice how it feels to bask in this love. Feel yourself rest in the love of a Lover God who promises to care for your every need and give you much more than you could ever dare to expect.

3

SURRENDER
AND OBEDIENCE

Christianity puts surrender to love right at the core of the spiritual journey. In order for us to understand exactly what that involves, we need to examine more carefully this concept of surrender.

A long time ago there was a young girl who was as unremarkable as the village in which she lived. Her name was Miriam—a common name in her country at the time. Her family were nothing special, and as far as those who knew her could tell, neither was she. To all appearances, she was just another impoverished teenager destined for obscurity in a remote village of an unimportant country at what seemed an insignificant point in human history.

Neither Miriam nor her family was particularly religious, although they were people of faith. There was no temple in their village, and religious teachers seldom visited their region. Miriam had, however, grown up hearing the stories of the heroes of their people and their great trust in God. One—the man they honored as the first of their tribe—"heard" God call him to leave his family and country and follow God to an unknown destination that was promised to be a place of great blessing. Immediately he did exactly that. And, according to the story, God kept his side of the bargain and greatly blessed him.

Stories of God's goodness were common in Miriam's community, legends of people who had placed their trust in God and not been disappointed. But God hadn't been heard from for a long time. Nobody in the village could remember a time when anyone they knew had been asked by God to exercise the sort of trust they communally valued.

All that changed when one day, completely out of the blue, an angel appeared to Miriam and told her that God had chosen her for an extremely special task. Miriam's first reaction was fear. Sensing this, the angel assured her that there was no reason to be afraid.

Fear then shifted to incredulity as the angel continued to speak. God—the angel said—had selected her to be the mother of his Son, a child who would be conceived by her union with God's Spirit. Instantly Miriam's head was flooded with a thousand questions. Once again fear crept in as she recognized a few of the implications of what was being proposed. But trust in the utterly dependable goodness of God was Miriam's deepest and surest instinct, and it didn't take more than an instant for her to make her reply: "I am the handmaid of the Lord," she said. "Let what you have said be done to me" (Luke 1:38).

Miriam, of course, is better known to us by her English name, Mary. Christians honor this humble Jewish young woman for her deep and unshakable trust in God and submission to his will. They honor her for her openness to God—trusting God to do with her as he chose. They honor her for her willingness to receive Jesus and allow him to live out his life within her. And they understand these qualities as illustrating surrender to divine love.

Surrender goes against the grain of autonomy and self-control. Under any circumstances other than trustworthy love, it may be extremely unwise. But in response to Perfect Love personally known, resistance can quickly dissipate and surrender become effortless—almost natural.

The surrender Jesus invites from us—choosing his will and his life over our own—can never be motivated by anything but love. But we can and frequently do offer a substitute for surrender— something that looks superficially enough like it that we easily confuse it with surrender. We can offer *obedience*.

CHOOSING TO OBEY

For many Christians, obedience is more familiar than surrender. The Bible never ever uses the term *surrender* apart from a military context, while it repeatedly encourages obedience. Not surprisingly, therefore, sermons and popular Christian writing typically also focus on obedience.

By contrasting obedience and surrender I do not want to put too much distance between them. Those who surrender obey. But not all who obey surrender. It is quite easy to obey God for the wrong reasons. What God desires is submission of our heart and will, not simply compliance in our behavior.

"Trust and obey" sums up the understanding of the Christian life of people who focus on obedience as an act of the will rather than a surrender of the heart. It suggests that all we have to do is believe certain things about God and then get on with doing what

God asks. While obedience may be demanding, we are tempted to think that it is achievable if we put our mind to it and are prepared for lots of hard work.

There are two problems with this. The first is that doing what God asks is, of course, not something we can ever achieve in ourselves. Not only did God never mean us to do so, he intended that our failures in obedience lead us to surrender. Rather than drive us to ever-increasing efforts to get it right ourselves, God wants our sin to make us aware of our need of him. This is what Paul meant by God's strength being made perfect in his weakness and was the reason he felt he should boast of his weaknesses (2 Corinthians 12:1-10). This is what Richard Rohr calls the spirituality of imperfection.[1]

The second problem in simply trying to do what God asks is that it leaves the kingdom of self intact. I remain in control, and my willful ways of running my life remain unchallenged. The whole point of the kingdom of God is to overturn the kingdom of self. These are the two rival spiritual kingdoms. We need to be very suspicious when self-control and egocentricity are left unchallenged in our Christ-following.

This does not mean, of course, that obedience is not a good thing. It is a Christian virtue, an extremely important one. Our well-being depends on obeying God. God's commandments are not arbitrary. They are like the manufacturer's handbook. Only a fool ignores them, as they tell us how life operates. They guide us to true life and to our deepest fulfillment.

Obedience is closely related to authority. To obey is to submit to the authority of someone. If we follow the maintenance recommendations in the manual of a new car, we accept the authority of the manufacturer. If we obey the laws of the land, we acknowledge the authority of the state. If we obey the laws of God, we submit to the authority of God.

This is the core of the biblical understanding of obedience. Obedience is submission to God's authority. When the winds and the sea submit to Christ's authority, they are described as obeying him (Matthew 8:27). The same is true of both unclean spirits (Mark 1:27) and human beings (1 Samuel 15:22). The Greek word our Bibles translate as "obey" suggests listening to God's will and submitting to it. Obedience is surrender to the authority that liberates us. Disobedience is refusing to submit to this authority.

It is clear, however, that God does not want mere behavioral compliance. He wants obedience in both conduct and heart. He wants us to do the right thing for the right reason. This is the phrase the author of Romans uses in describing the goal of Christian spirituality as to be "obedient from the heart" (Romans 6:17 NASB).

In fact, obedience that does not flow from the heart counts for very little in the eyes of God. It's what's inside that counts. Motivation counts because God wants our love and friendship, not just the right behavior. If he simply wanted compliance, he could have created a race of automatons. But desiring communion with beings enough like him to make intimacy possible, he created humans. And he patiently woos us as we learn not just to do what he desires but to surrender to his love.

This is made particularly clear in Jesus' teaching in the Sermon on the Mount. If we have been hoping to meet God's minimal standards through compliance with the letter of the law, this sermon contains some extremely discouraging news. For here Jesus raises the bar by asserting that righteousness is a matter of both heart and conduct. He reminds us that God wants our heart, not just our will.

WILLFUL OR WILLING?

To rely on the will for Christian obedience is to reinforce our natural willful self-determination. This lies right at the core of our egocentricity, something that no human has to be taught. Just watch the nearest two-year-old if you have any doubt about the strength of willfulness.

Relying on the will to make things happen keeps us focused on the self. Life lived with resolve and determination is life lived apart from surrender. It is living with clenched-fisted doggedness. It is living the illusion that I can be in control. It is the rule of life lived in the kingdom of self.

Willingness, on the other hand, involves release of control. Symbolized by open hands, it is the surrender of my autonomy and my will. It is giving up my illusory quest for control. And it is relinquishment of the keys to the kingdom of self.

Christ is the epitome of life lived with willingness. "Your will be done," he prayed in what we call the Lord's Prayer (Matthew 6:10). And more than just in prayer, he *lived* this posture of preferring God's will to his own. Christian spirituality is following Christ in this self-abandonment. It is following his example of willing surrender.

Obedience that is the grudging fruit of willful determination does not give God any more pleasure than it gives a parent. Nor does it bring us the vitality and fulfillment for which we long. All it does is reinforce our egocentricity and make us more rigid and more proud.

Obedience that flows from a surrendered heart is totally different. Rather than willpower and resolve, love is the motive for what we will and what we do. This is the pattern of genuine Christian spiritual transformation. Such transformation always works from the inside out. And love is always its source, motivation and expression.

WILLING TO SURRENDER

If the core of Christian obedience is listening to God's will, the core of surrender is voluntarily giving up our will. Only love can induce us to do this. But even more remarkable, not only can love make it possible, it can make it almost easy.

Surrender to anything other than love would be idiocy. Alarm bells should go off when we hear of people surrendering to abusive relationships. Surrender involves too much vulnerability to be a responsible action in relation to anything other than unconditional love. Ultimately, of course, this means that absolute surrender can only be offered to Perfect Love. Only God deserves absolute surrender, because only God can offer absolutely dependable love.

In spite of our natural resistance to submission, deep within the human soul there seems to be a yearning to surrender. Although it does not fit with the image I usually want to project, all my life I have longed to give myself completely to someone or something bigger than myself. This lies right at the heart of what it means to be human. We are creatures made in the image of God, and Spirit calls to spirit, reminding us that there is no freedom apart from surrender.

But being made in the image of God means that to fail to find our freedom in surrender to God is inevitably to experience frustration and disappointment. No other love is worthy of our surrender. No other cause is big enough. Surrender to lesser gods will always become a source of bondage, not a spring of vitality.

Jesus is the key to surrender to God. He does not command us

to surrender or wield authority to demand obedience. Instead he
welcomes us with love that invites intimacy. Rather than com-
manding with power, he invites with vulnerability. In Jesus, God
becomes human and courts us with tenderness and unimaginable
kindness. He does so because he wants our heart and not just our
will. He knows that only love will make us willing to give him both
our heart and our will.

Jesus invites us to come to him and relinquish the control of our
life. He invites us to give up our desperate and illusory striving after autonomy. He also invites us to abandon the isolation and rigidity associated with our egocentricity. And in their place he
offers rest, fulfillment, and the discovery of our true and deepest
self in Christ. When we take this step of surrender, we suddenly
discover the place for which we have been unconsciously longing.
Like a tool seized by a strong hand, we are at last where we belong;
we know we have been found.

Paradoxically, the abundant life promised us in Christ comes
not from grasping but from releasing. It comes not from striving
but from relinquishing. It comes not so much from taking as from
giving. Surrender is the foundational dynamic of Christian freedom—surrender of my efforts to live my life outside of the grasp
of God's love and surrender to God's will and gracious Spirit.

Surrender is being willing rather than willful. It is a readiness to
trust that is based in love. It is relaxing and letting go. It is floating
in the river that is God's love.

FLOATING AS SURRENDER

I recently had a fascinating experience teaching some people how
to swim. A group of spiritual directors I was working with in the
Philippines came with my wife and me to the beach for a few days

of holiday. All were considerably more advanced on the spiritual journey than in their swimming skills. In fact, all were complete nonswimmers, and all had some degree of terror of the water. But it was remarkable how quickly they learned to swim. Within an hour of first entering the water wearing life jackets, having just released their white-knuckled grip of the sides of the boat, all of them had abandoned the life vests and were snorkeling on their own in the ocean. How could this be possible?

The key was not skilful instruction. The key was that they had already grasped the spiritual principle of surrender, that we already had a relationship of trust, and that they were willing to enter the water and let go of the side of the boat.

They trusted me when I told them that they would float, and lo and behold, when they took off their life vests and lay back in the water, they did just that. And they trusted me when I told them that they could breathe through the snorkel without having to lift their heads out of the water, and lo and behold, this also proved true. They had learned to surrender to God, so learning to trust in this situation was relatively easy.

With delight one woman exclaimed, "Nobody told me that you don't have to do anything to float!" She made a more profound spiritual point than she realized.

The English word *surrender* carries the implication of putting one's full weight on someone or something. It involves letting go—a release of effort, tension and fear. And it involves trust. One cannot let go of self-dependence and transfer dependence to someone else without trust.

Floating is a good illustration of this, because you cannot float until you let go. Floating is putting your full weight on the water and trusting that you will be supported. It is letting go of your natural instincts to fight against sinking. Only then do you discover that you are supported.

GOING WITH THE FLOW

It is interesting that the apostle John describes the Spirit as a stream of flowing water, a spring welling up inside us (John 4:10-14). This same image is repeated in Revelation, where we encounter the river of life that flows from the throne of God and from the Lamb (Revelation 22:1-2).

Richard Rohr notes that "faith might be precisely that ability to trust the river, to trust the flow and the lover. . . . There is a river. The river is flowing; we are in it. The river is God's providential love."[2] The reason we do not have to be afraid is that we have been given the Spirit of God. We are in the river. We do not need to thrash about trying to float.

Early Christian writers often imaged the Christian life in terms of living in water like a fish. Tertullian called Christ the "Heavenly Fish" and Christians "little fish" who take their name from *Ichthus* (fish).[3] Christians, according to these writers, are born and live within the divine waters of the Spirit. The Christian life is learning to be supported by these waters.

An ancient Sufi story speaks of fish that spend their days anxiously swimming around in search of water, failing to realize that they are in the midst of it. Their distress is suddenly eliminated when they open their eyes and see where they really are.

One of the women in the group of spiritual directors who were learning to swim did have a problem. Her biggest challenge was letting go of seeing where she was. She was afraid that while she was floating she might run into something, so she kept lifting her head out of the water to look around. Each time she did so, she began to sink.

So it is with us. We need to stop searching and see that we are surrounded by the sea of Perfect Love. But we also need to stop our panicky thrashing about in an effort to float. Paradoxically, our efforts to stay afloat usually lead to sinking. Every time we start to panic and think we need to do something to stay afloat, we lift our head out of the water and no longer rest in it. As soon as we do we begin to sink. Our efforts to stay afloat may keep our head above the water for a while, but eventually we tire, and eventually our efforts to keep afloat will drown us.

The woman who raised her head reminds me of how quickly we get nervous when we stop to observe how our floating is going. For as soon as we stop and observe our floating, we're overcome by an automatic impulse to do something to keep afloat. We start thrashing about. Like Peter, who began to sink as soon as he observed himself walking on the water, we begin to sink as soon as we begin to worry about how the floating is going. Our efforts to stay afloat—that is, our efforts to earn God's love—are always counterproductive. We must simply open our spiritual eyes and see that we are in the river of God's love and that our staying afloat and moving along are God's responsibility. All we have to do is surrender.

We float only when we stop trying to do so. And we never discover that we do not need to do anything to stay afloat until we let go. That is surrender.

Surrender is the discovery that we are in a river of love and that we float without having to do anything. Apart from such surrender, we always are in the grip of some degree of fear. Apart from such surrender, we will always thrash about, trying to stay afloat by our own efforts. And apart from such surrender, we remain self-preoccupied as our willful attempts to stay in control cut us off from life itself.

CHRISTIAN OBEDIENCE AND SURRENDER

Christian obedience should always be based on surrender to a person, not simply acceptance of an obligation. It is surrender to love, not submission to a duty.

Too often people see Christianity in terms of rules and morality—a system of obligations and prohibitions. This entirely misses the point of Christ-following. Christian obedience is more like what lovers give each other than what soldiers give their superiors. Lovers demonstrate their love by doing what each other wants. And so it should be with Christians and their God.

Far from being incompatible with obedience, surrender provides the motive for obedience. We should obey God because he has won our hearts in love. If he has not, our focus should not be so much on obedience as on knowing his love. For once we get that solidly in place, obedience begins to take care of itself.

Apart from love, obedience is simply an act of obligation. As a response to love, duty becomes an act of devotion. God wants our devotion, not simply our acts of duty.

Exploring the role of surrender in Christian spirituality, Francis de Sales distinguishes between two aspects of the will of God—what he calls God's "signified will" and the "will of his good pleasure."[4]

God's "signified will" is what he commands. And it's surprising how short the list of commands actually is. When we start cataloging the things we think God demands, we usually come up with quite a long list. But God gave Moses a list of only ten items. Jesus reduced it to two—love of God and love of our neighbor (Mark 12:30). This is the signified will of God. Christians seek to obey this, aware, however, that we cannot do so on our own. God's signified will should therefore drive us back to him as we encounter our inability to do what he desires.

While God's "signified will" invites the surrender of active obedience, the "will of God's good pleasure" invites a more passive, gentle surrender. Through it God invites us to yield to his way, to prefer his way to our own. He invites us to learn to prefer his reign over our life to our own reign. Surrender to the "will of God's good pleasure" is, according to Francis, trust in God's love.

Christ perfectly illustrates both forms of surrender. He submitted himself to God's authority and perfectly did as God commanded. This was his active surrender to God's revealed will. But he went beyond this. He also trusted the will of God's good pleasure, choosing and trusting God's love and resting confidently in God's will.

Both Moses and Job also illustrate surrender to God. Neither simply obeyed in acts of willfulness. But the differences between their responses to God illustrate the two forms of surrender described by Francis.

Moses' encounter with God in the burning bush illustrates surrender to God's signified will. God told Moses to go back to Egypt and set his people free. Moses obeyed. His surrender was active, not passive or resigned. He left the wilderness, traveled back to Egypt and told Pharaoh why he had come. There wasn't anything passive about his response. His surrender involved commitment and action.

Job faced a different situation, and his response demonstrates surrender to the will of God's good pleasure. Job, you will recall, was facing devastating personal disasters that he had neither chosen nor caused. The surrender God asked of him was surrender to the trustworthiness of God's will. This is the surrender of ultimate dependence.

Surrender and obedience are closely related. The surrender God desires begins in the heart and expresses itself in behavior. It involves both an active embracing of God's designated will and a passive acceptance of his permissive will. Knowing the trustworthiness of his love is the foundation of both.

WHEN SURRENDER IS HARDER THAN IT SOUNDS

Difficulties in obedience or surrender are often viewed as problems of the will. This is the reason some Christians try over and over again to "surrender all," each time attempting to do so with more fervor and resolve. But this misses the point of surrendering first to love and allowing obedience to be an obligation of love, not a response to a commandment.

Ultimately, problems in surrender and obedience are problems of knowing God's love. They are problems therefore of the heart, not the will.

Christian surrender is saying yes to God's *Yes!* to me. It begins as I experience his wildly enthusiastic, recklessly loving affirmation of me. It grows out of soaking myself in this love so thoroughly that love for God springs up in response. Surrender to his love is the work of his Spirit, making his love ours and his nature ours. This is the core of Christian spiritual transformation.

Angie, the woman who reacted so strongly to my use of the term *surrender,* found herself being drawn into surrender to the God she had feared as she became utterly convinced that God loved her as she was and with unimaginable extravagance. God turned out to be far different from what she had imagined—gentle, never keeping a record of her failures and exquisitely concerned about her deepest fulfillment. God turned out to be much more like a lover than an authority figure.

St. Ignatius of Loyola notes that sin is unwillingness to trust that what God wants is our deepest happiness. Until I am absolutely convinced of this I will do everything I can to keep my hands on the controls of my life, because I think I know better than God what I need for my fulfillment.

Surrender to God flows out of the experience of love that will never let me go. It is the response of the heart that knows that since God is for me, nothing can come between me and the perfect love that surrounds me and will support me regardless of my effort, my response or even my attention.

Considering how easy and natural floating is, I am amazed how much energy I expend treading water. The lie I seem to believe is that my efforts are keeping me afloat, perhaps even keep me moving through the water. The reality is that all they do is tire me out, hold me in the same place and deprive me of the joyous discovery that I am supported.

How like the anxious fish in the Sufi legend I often am—swimming to and fro, hunting for the water that in actuality surrounds and sustains me.

It is no wonder that I long for rest. Trying to stay afloat and move through the water on my own energy satisfies my willful sense of independence, but it leaves me exhausted. And I never seem to get where I think I should be going.

Then, in exhaustion, I momentarily surrender. I relax. I allow my full weight to be supported by the Spirit. And not only do I float, I flow with the current. I hadn't even been aware that there was a current. My thrashing about in the water made me oblivious to its presence and force. Now I begin to know what I was fighting.

To fail to go with the flow is to try to push the river. But the river—God's Spirit—does not need any help.

FOR FURTHER REFLECTION

Perhaps something within you is sighing in response to these images and words. Perhaps you too are tired from fighting to stay afloat. The effort of obedience is beginning to wear you down. The bleak gray of dutiful resolve and determination is beginning to depress you. The hint of the warm colors of surrender to love enliven your longings as they begin to appear on your horizon.

If so, I encourage you to set the book down and listen to those longings. They are the call of Spirit to spirit. They are the whisper of God's still small voice within—a voice that invites you to know how deeply loved you are and to surrender to that love. They are an invitation to trust that obedience can and will spring from love, not simply from obligation. They are the call of the Cosmic Lover to his beloved.

Revisit any of the meditations at the end of the first two chapters that communicated that love to you, personally and directly. Allow them to speak to you again. And then trust yourself to that love.

Surrender to love is never a once-for-all done deal. I surrender, and then I lift my head out of the water to see where I am or where I am going. Immediately I start to tread water again. Then again I must surrender. I must trust that I am supported.

There is no reason to feel guilty if you need to hear the invitation to surrender over and over again, each time responding with whatever surrender you can offer at the moment. Guilt only complicates surrender, leading to more thrashing about. Whenever I discover that I have slipped out of surrender and back into my treading-water mode, I need to simply relax and allow the river of love to again support me. Time wasted on slapping my wrist and wringing my hands is time when I could be floating.

In summary, meditate on the familiar words of a great spiritual floater—St. Paul. As you do, remember that this was the willful man who doggedly persecuted Christians out of religious fervor. How did he learn willing surrender? He encountered Perfect Love. Listen to Paul talk about the great love of his life, and allow yourself to be buoyed up by it:

> After saying this, what can we add? With God on our side who can be against us? Since God did not spare his own Son, but gave him up to benefit us all, we may be certain, after such a gift, that he will not refuse anything he can give. Could anyone accuse those that God has chosen? When God acquits, could anyone condemn? Could Christ Jesus? No! He not only died for us—he rose from the dead, and there at God's right hand he stands and pleads for us.
>
> Nothing therefore can come between us and the love of Christ, even if we are troubled or worried, or being persecuted, or lacking food or clothes, or being threatened or even attacked. . . . For I am certain of this: neither death nor life, no angel, no prince, nothing that exists, nothing still to come, not any power, or height or depth, nor any created thing, can ever come between us and the love of God made visible in Christ Jesus our Lord. (Romans 8:31-39)

Know this love as yours, and float!

4

TRANSFORMED BY LOVE

Transformation is a big concept, not simply a big word. It involves change on a grand scale—bigger than most of us know much about from personal experience.

Typically our experience of personal change is limited to small, incremental shifts that are visible mainly in retrospect. Perhaps as I look back it may appear that I have begun to control my temper better or be a little more disciplined about food. But while changes of this sort are important, they pale in significance when compared to the notion of transformation. In fact, they tend to make the idea of fundamental makeover seem extravagantly unrealistic.

However, if we dare to be honest, we all know our need for radical change. We know the immense difference between our outward appearance and inner reality. Our love is more self-serving than it appears, our woundedness deeper, our self-deceptions more pernicious. Our failures to live up to even our own expectations and ideals are massive. Our failures to live up to God's expectations are profound.

Jesus knew this. This is why his call to leave everything, follow him and experience true life is so striking. It puts us in touch with the reality of our inner world, and it makes us aware of the depth of our longing for real change. So unlike the message of self-improvement gurus who offer the small extra bits of help we think we need to finish off our personal renovation projects, Jesus' offer is abundant life based on death and rebirth. Change doesn't get much more radical than that!

The language of transformation is too optimistic for psychology. At one time psychotherapists dared to use the bold language of cure. With more modesty, most now speak of aiding growth. Some simply think in terms of helping adjustment and coping.

But the language of transformation is profoundly Christian. Paul reminds us that the goal of the spiritual journey is being transformed into the image of God—the image we were created to reflect (2 Corinthians 3:18). Christian transformation never settles for cosmetic adjustments. It involves being reborn—remade into who we were destined from eternity to be.

But recall who Paul was and what his authority is to speak of personal transformation. We pick up his story when he was known by another name.

Saul was the champion of a reign of terror against Christians in the early days of the church. With unrelenting zeal he committed his life to hunting down and killing those who followed Jesus. Fueled by hatred and fanaticism, he set as his mission the elimination of every trace of Christianity from first-century Palestine.

How little he could have guessed what lay in store for him when one day he set out to go to Damascus, "breathing threats to slaughter the Lord's disciples" (Acts 9:1). This day did not find him in the midst of a self-improvement program to which Christian conversion might add a helpful component. This day found him self-preoccupied with his hatred and in the grip of his tyrannical rigidity. It was, for him, a typical day.

"Suddenly, while he was traveling to Damascus and just before he reached the city, there came a light from heaven all around him. He fell to the ground, and then he heard a voice saying, 'Saul, Saul, why are you persecuting me?' 'Who are you, Lord?' he asked, and the voice answered, 'I am Jesus'" (Acts 9:3-5).

This was just the beginning of the changes that led to the death of Saul and the birth of Paul—a man who was to become as famous for his love of Christ and his followers as Saul had been for his hatred. This was the beginning of the end of his arrogance, and the end of his self-preoccupation. This would turn out to be his first day of real life. It was nothing short of conversion—a rebirth.

If Paul has something to say about transformation, we should listen. He spoke from personal experience!

THE TRANSFORMATIONAL JOURNEY

The Chinese philosopher Lao Tzu reminds us that even a journey of a thousand miles must begin with a single step. What, then, is the first step on the Christian transformational journey?

Christians have applied a variety of words to this first step— *conversion, purgation, repentance,* to name but a few. Jesus also referred to the first step with a variety of terms. Sometimes he encouraged people to repent of their sins. Other times he asked them to follow him. And sometimes he simply asked them to allow him to heal them. All seemed to invite the same response—

death to their old kingdom of self and an awakening of a new life of surrender to Perfect Love.

Stepping onto the road of Christian spiritual transformation requires an encounter with the living God. This encounter may be gradual or it may be sudden. But it will always involve a turning and an awakening.

Turning is repentance. Repentance, however, is never simply turning *from* something—sin or a way of life. It must also always involve turning *to* something. Christian repentance is turning to Jesus.

Mary Magdalene's experience at Jesus' tomb on the morning of the resurrection provides a striking image of such a turning (John 20:11-18). Picture the moment.

Mary is standing outside the tomb. She is overcome with grief. But worse, she is bewildered and frightened. The dramatic events of the last several days flash through her mind. She feels again the stab of pain on recalling that Jesus—the One who had given her back her life—had been killed. It felt as if her life had ended with his.

Now she has discovered that his body has been taken from the grave. This only adds to her agony. She weeps. It is all she can do.

Suddenly she is joined by someone she assumes to be the gardener. And then the stranger speaks one simple word—her name. Instantly she recognizes the voice. It is the same voice that had assured her of his love. It is the voice of her beloved—Jesus.

In an instant Mary turns from despair to hope. Pain turns to joy, and life surges again through her body and spirit.

The essence of Mary's turning was repentance—turning toward Jesus and accepting the gifts of his love. But Mary also illustrates spiritual awakening. First she turned toward Jesus, and then she recognized him. It was the recognition that brought her back to life. But first she had to turn toward him. When she recognized him, her eyes were suddenly opened—not just her physical eyes of recognition but her spiritual eyes of awareness. Suddenly she remembered how deeply loved she was. And suddenly she knew that she was not alone. Never again could they take her Lord from her. Never again could she be alone. For she had been reunited with the Lover of her soul.

Turning toward Jesus is the heart of repentance, because this is the only real possibility of turning away from sin. Turning toward Jesus also makes clear that repentance must be an ongoing matter. It must become a way of life.

Jesus' call to each one of us is a call to be aware of his presence, to turn toward him and to surrender to his love. This is the call he offers me each and every day of my life. My response is never once for all. As Anthony of the Desert said, "Every morning I must say again to myself, today I start."[1]

Conversion is the lifelong transformational process of being remade into the image of God. It is so much more than simply trying to avoid sin. The focus of repentance and conversion is Jesus, not my sin nor my self.

My attachment to sinful ways of being is much too strong to ever be undone by mere willpower. There is no substitute for surrender to divine love as the fuel to propel such undoing. Divine love transforms both my heart and my will. Divine love enables me to choose God's will over mine. Without this, repentance will be nothing more than a self-help scheme based on effort and resolve.

Christian conversion is the most radical change process in human history. So much more than a mere change of the externals of our life, it is the refashioning of our entire being. The scope of transformation it entails makes even the most extravagant claims of therapeutic psychology pale by comparison.

But if an encounter with divine love is really so transformational, how is it that so many of us have survived such encounters relatively unchanged? It seems that the experience of love—even God's love—does not always have transforming consequences. It is important to understand why this is the case if we are to allow ourselves to meet divine love in ways that lead to genuine change.

THE NAKED SELF

The single most important thing I have learned in over thirty years of study of how love produces healing is that love is transformational only when it is received in vulnerability.

Suppose that with God's help I am able to love my son unconditionally. But if he is desperately trying to please me, the unconditional nature of my love will not be noticed. And there will be no deep experience of knowing himself deeply and unconditionally loved. Receiving love while he is trying to earn it will only reinforce his efforts to be lovable. Far from being transformational, this will only increase his efforts to earn love. And any love he receives will only be experienced as the fruit of these efforts.

Genuine transformation requires vulnerability. It is not the fact of being loved unconditionally that is life-changing. It is the risky experience of *allowing myself* to be loved unconditionally.

Paradoxically, no one can change until they first accept themselves as they are. Self-deceptions and an absence of real vulnerability block any meaningful transformation. It is only when I accept who I am that I dare to show you that self in all its vulnerability and nakedness. Only then do I have the opportunity to receive your love in a manner that makes a genuine difference.

This applies equally to God's love and the love of other people.

Psychoanalyst George Benson describes it as receiving love in an undefended state. He suggests that willingness to receive the love of God and others without earning it is at the heart of both psychological and spiritual growth. I think he is correct. Speaking of the openness to divine love that results in transformation, Benson warns that "it is foolish to move in this fearful direction unless you are motivated by a private yearning for the presence of God; unless you sense the aching deficit within you that cannot be made right by clever maneuvers. If you can believe that you've 'got it made' or that the 'good life' is just ahead of you, forget transformation and scrap the Christian faith."[2]

Daring to accept myself and receive love for who I am in my nakedness and vulnerability is the indispensable precondition for genuine transformation. But make no mistake about just how difficult this is. Everything within me wants to show my best "pretend self" to both other people and God. This is my false self—the self of my own making. This self can never be transformed, because it is never willing to receive love in vulnerability. When this pretend self receives love, it simply becomes stronger and I am even more deeply in bondage to my false ways of living.

Both popular psychology and spirituality—even popular Christian spirituality—tend to reinforce this false self by playing to our deep-seated belief in self-improvement. Both also play to our instinctual tendency to attempt to get our act together by ourselves before we receive love.

The life and message of Jesus stand diametrically opposed to such efforts at self-improvement. Jesus did not come to encourage our self-transformation schemes. He understood that rather than longing to receive his love in an undefended state, what we really want is to manipulate God to accept us in our false and defended ways of being. If only he would do this, we could remain unaware of just how desperately we need real love.

How terrifying it is to face my naked and needy self—the self that longs for love and knows it can do nothing to manipulate the universe into providing the only kind of love I really need. The crux of the problem is that I cannot feel the love of God because I do not dare to accept it unconditionally. To know that I am loved, I must accept the frightening helplessness and vulnerability that is my true state. This is always terrifying.

BEYOND BELIEF

But speaking practically, how are we to know God's love in a way that meets us in these deepest parts of our vulnerable self? How can we ever come to know that God's love is, in fact, genuinely unconditional?

The knowing of God's love that most Christians content themselves with is what I have called objective rather than personal knowing. We believe in God's love, just as we believe other articles of faith. Since such belief is strongly supported by Scripture, we correctly assume that it is trustworthy. And it is. But we may also assume that it is sufficient. And it is not.

Gerald May calls the sort of knowing of love that is essential for transformation "contemplative knowing." We could also describe it as *experiential knowing*. It is a knowing that has moved beyond belief to experience. It is a knowing that can be tested by both reason and belief, but it is not a product of either. It is, May states, "a knowing that grows within one's heart and directs the very substance of one's life. . . . There is no leap of faith into this knowing. Contemplative knowing involves a leap—some would say a quantum leap—beyond faith."[3]

This is the only knowing of love that is strong enough to cast out fear. And this is the only knowing of love that is capable of offering us the radical transformation we need. Mere belief is simply not strong enough to do the job. Relying on belief leaves me clinging to the things I believe. And there is always the threat of doubt, which seems to hold the potential of opening the back door and allowing fear to reenter.

What we need is a knowing that is deeper than belief. It must be based on experience. Only knowing love is sufficiently strong to cast out fear. Only knowing love is sufficiently strong to resist doubt.

The reason May calls such knowing "contemplative" is that it results from meeting God in a contemplative state. It comes from sitting at the feet of Jesus, gazing into his face and listening to his assurances of love for me. It comes from letting God's love wash over me, not simply trying to believe it. It comes from soaking in the scriptural assurances of such love, not simply reading them and trying to remember or believe them. It comes from spending time with God, observing how he looks at me. It comes from watching his watchfulness over me and listening to his protestations of love for me.

Because such knowing is beyond faith, it is more immune to doubt. Just as the child who regularly meets her mother's love in the core of her being knows that love without any effort to believe it to be true, so we may know God's love in a way that is deeper and more durable than knowing based on belief. Contemplative or existential knowing may be supported by belief, but it is never reducible to it. It is based in experience, the direct personal encounter with divine love. The goal is, as stated by Paul, that we might know the love of Christ, which is beyond all knowledge, and so be filled with the utter fullness of God (Ephesians 3:16-19).

Undefended Snuggling

Amanda and her mother illustrate the transformational nature of receiving love in vulnerability.

Amanda was fifteen when she was referred to me after a serious suicidal attempt. It was her third attempt in as many months, each becoming more serious. The first had occurred just after her boyfriend hung himself. She had found his body and made a vow that she would join him in death.

When I first met her in the waiting room, Amanda was dressed head to toe in black, with large black circles painted around her eyes. Her face and ears were riddled with studs and rings, and she wore a dog collar and tag. The collar was attached to a waist belt with a conspicuous industrial-grade chain. Chains also dangled from the epaulets of her black trench coat. I recognized the uniform of a goth—that role prized by angry young people because of its enormous potential to shock.

Amanda did not even acknowledge my presence when I introduced myself. She did, however, get up and follow me to my office. I was somewhat surprised that the woman sitting beside her did the same. In my office, she introduced herself as Amanda's mother. Turning to Amanda I asked if she was willing to have her mother accompany her for this consultation. She answered that her mother was her best friend and that she had come because she was invited.

I was intrigued. Young people like Amanda are not often best friends with their mothers. And yet the affection between them was clear. Sensing also, however, her mother's disapproval of Amanda's lifestyle, I asked what was the bond that had allowed her to remain close to her mother. Amanda replied, "For as long as I can remember, every night of my life I end the day by getting in bed with my mother and snuggling."

Amanda's relationship with her mother is quite remarkable, and is in large part responsible for the fact that she has now left behind what she describes as her "black period" and is finding her way through adolescence in a relatively healthy manner. Amanda knew that she was deeply loved just exactly as she was. Her mother disapproved of her use of drugs, her promiscuous sex, her astoundingly profane language, her Satanic practices and most other aspects of her lifestyle. But with a wisdom that I have rarely seen in parents, she recognized that what her daughter needed was not lectures but love. Fortunately, she had been giving this in large doses for all of Amanda's life. Equally fortunately, she did not now allow her disapproval of her daughter's behavior to interrupt this pattern in the slightest.

Amanda's mother offered a truly transforming love—transforming because while it could be resisted, it could not be received without profound psychospiritual impact.

ENCOUNTERING DIVINE LOVE

The key to spiritual transformation is meeting God—as Amanda met her mother—in vulnerability. Our natural inclination is to bring the most presentable parts of our self to the encounter with God. But God wants us to bring our whole self to the divine encounter. He wants us to trust him enough to meet Perfect Love in the vulnerability of our shame, weakness and sin.

Trevor Hudson describes conversion as "a continuing process that unfolds one day at a time as we bring more and more of ourselves to God."[4] Tragically, however, most of us have large tracts of our inner world that are excluded from God's transforming love and friendship. Perpetuating such exclusions limits our conversion. It is like going to the doctor for a checkup and denying any problems, focusing only on the parts of oneself that are most healthy. As Christ himself said, the healthy have no need of a physician. He came to save the sick and sinful (Matthew 9:12).

Jesus' parable about the banquet illustrates this process meeting God in our places of vulnerability. In Luke 14:15-24 Jesus compares the kingdom of God to a great feast. Many people are invited, but all make excuses for not coming. At the last minute, therefore, the host sends his servants out into the streets and alleys of the town, telling them to bring in the poor, crippled, blind and lame. He makes special places for them at his feast.

Hudson notes that one level of interpretation of this parable is to see it as describing the process of inner transformation. Think of Christ as presiding over a banquet at the deep center of our being. His invitation to us is to search out the poor, crippled, blind and lame aspects of our inner self and bring them to his feast of love. Here he stands ready to embrace them with love and welcome them into the family of self that he is slowly weaving together in the ongoing transformation of our life.

What a shame, therefore, when we turn up at the banquet with our most spiritual parts of self, leaving the other parts that really need healing and transformation hidden in the darkness of our depths. "Denying our shadow selves access to the banquet hinders our ongoing conversion, splits our lives dangerously, and renders us vulnerable to what we have denied."[5]

Transformation occurs when we bring all parts of ourselves into the banquet of love provided by our divine host. Our fearful, angry and wounded parts of self can never be healed unless they are exposed to divine love. This is why we must meet God's love in our vulnerability and brokenness, not simply in our strength and togetherness. Only as we do so can our damaged and infirm parts of self be exposed to transforming love.

Transformation demands that we meet God in the vulnerability of our sin and shame rather than retreating to try to get on with our self-improvement projects. But it also requires that we stay long enough in his loving presence to allow our shame to begin to melt away. For love to transform us, not only must we meet in vulnerability, we must also linger long enough for it to penetrate our woundedness. Snuggling keeps us in contact with love long enough that it has that effect.

ALL LOVE IS GOD'S LOVE

The more perfect the love, the more it forces us to encounter our own fear. For this reason we sometimes prefer to meet love in safer places. This easily leads to confusing our longings for divine and human love, so that we expect unconditional love from human beings. Most people probably do this at some point or another on their journey. Some never find their way out of this cul de sac.

Romantic love is especially easily confused with divine love, particularly during its moments of flaming passion. The desire for union that emerges from romantic love often makes it hard to separate the ultimate surrender that one longs for in relation to God from the penultimate surrender that one appropriately gives to a human lover. But when the passion dies down, confusion of divine and romantic love can lead to great disappointment. Investing hopes that can be fulfilled only by God in human beings always has this potential.

But it is not just lovers who can mistakenly expect perfect love from humans. Friends can do the same. Once again, the result will always be disappointment. Parents, similarly, are unable to carry the burden of offering perfect love to their children, as are children to their parents. This need can be met only in God.

The deep human longings for surrender to perfect love can never be satisfied by anyone other than God. Human love, no matter how noble, is always contaminated to some extent by self-interest. Narcissistic wounds—particularly if unacknowledged—will always limit the self-sacrificial qualities of unconditional love.

But although human beings can never offer perfect love, human love always carries enough of its source within it that it retains something of the healing and growth-inducing potential of divine love. Amanda's mother clearly demonstrates this. Love always contains sparks of divine presence. Where love is, God is—for God is love and love is of God (1 John 4:7-8). *Ubi caritas et amor, Deus ibi est*—where charity and love are, there is God.

This is why genuine love always calls us to deeper places of trust and connection. Even the love exchanged between people and their pets has health-inducing potential. It is not the pet that is the cause of the benefit but the cosmic presence of divine love—existing in the world as a reflection of the nature of the Creator and present in human beings as they bear his image.

While human love can never bear the weight of our need for divine love, it can support transformation and teach us about divine love. Human love communicates divine love. There is no other source of love but God. Experiences of human love bring us therefore into an indirect encounter with divine love. They also can serve to prepare us to respond to that love by making the idea of God's love believable. The relative constancy of the love of family and friends makes the absolute faithfulness of divine love at least conceivable. Hints of unconditional love from humans makes the possibility of absolutely unconditional divine love imaginable.

Human love also makes divine love trustworthy. Learning limited surrender to relatively trustworthy human beings helps prepare us for more complete surrender to perfect love. Tragically, however, the flip side of this is also true. Conditional and imperfect love from human beings makes the unconditional and perfect love of God seem unbelievable and untrustworthy.

Only perfect love can completely cast out fear. And since God alone is perfect love, there is no substitute for learning what love really is by coming back to the source. God is the original that shows up the limitations of all the copies. His love, and only his love, is capable of the deep transformation we desperately need. And as we shall see in the next chapter, his love and only his love is capable of making us into the great lovers he intends us to be.

Angie learned to trust God's love in part by learning to trust mine. Her life experiences had taught her to avoid any form of vulnerability. She despised weakness and saw anything that was soft or vulnerable as weak. Power she respected but feared. She placed God in the category of power, not weakness.

Initially she viewed me as someone powerful and responded with fear. But inevitably she discovered what I had known all along—that I had limitations and imperfections, in short, that I was human. I was not as smart as she, I would occasionally forget things she had told me, and I would from time to time get tired in a session. She pounced on any of these discoveries with rage and a feeling of betrayal. However, something kept her coming back. Later she told me it was the safety and consistency she felt I offered her. Slowly she came to accept my limitations. And she began to accept my acceptance of her. And slowly she became open to God.

What she discovered was that God was not at all like the god of her imagination. The biggest surprise was God's vulnerability.

It was this that made her most ready to receive his love. She had expected a God of power. What she found in the Christ of the Gospels was a God of weakness. It was the love of this weak and vulnerable God that was most transforming for her. For if God could dare to take risks in entering human life in vulnerability, perhaps she could take the risk he invited in meeting him in her weakness. She was finally ready to receive perfect love in an undefended state.

Only divine love is capable of effecting the transformation Angie experienced. Her relationship with me allowed her to first experience divine love indirectly. This helped her be ready for the real thing. As I told her, if she found anything safe and trustworthy in me, that was Jesus in me. It was God's love that slowly began to thaw her frozen and frightened spirit. It was Perfect Love that slowly awakened her own capacities for love.

FOR FURTHER REFLECTION

Take some time to think about the difference love makes in your life. Allow the following to help you do so.

- First reflect on a world without love—a world with human beings not made in the image of God and a world into which God did not enter or to which he did not reveal himself. Allow yourself to imagine the despair of life in such a world without love.

- Contrast this to the world in which you live. Allow the Spirit to bring to your mind the panorama of people who have loved you or prayed for you across your life. Think about what each has taught you about the nature of Perfect Love.

- Then reflect on the ways you have experienced God's love

directly and personally. Picture yourself soaking in this love, and notice what changes within you.

❧ Finally, ask God to help you identify ways you still hide from his love. Think of how you could spend more time snuggling with Jesus, allowing his love to heal your deepest pockets of shame and brokenness. Ask also for his help in identifying the weak and inferior parts of yourself that you are reluctant to invite into the banquet of love God wishes to host within you. And ask him to show you the next steps he wishes to lead you to on the transformational journey of surrender to Perfect Love.

5

BECOMING LOVE

In his meditation on Rembrandt's painting *The Return of the Prodigal Son,* Henri Nouwen notes that the reason we are invited to return to the love of the Father is to become like the Father.[1] Reflection on either the painting or the parable that inspired it makes it easy for most of us to identify with aspects of either the younger or older brother. We may see ourselves in the self-righteousness of the older brother or the pride and rebelliousness of the younger son. But are we also able to identify with the father?

The point of God's love is to remake us in his image of love. The point of the spiritual journey is not simply to be received back into the welcoming arms of love of the Father but to become like the Father. Jesus reminds us of this when he tells his followers to "be compassionate as your Father is compassionate" (Luke 6:36). God wants us to make his life ours, his heart ours, his love ours. He wants us to be—like him—characterized by love.

Nouwen notes that "becoming like the heavenly Father is not

just one important aspect of Jesus' teaching, it is the very heart of his message."[2] What God wants is daughters and sons who show a family resemblance. He wants us to be known as great lovers because love is his way.

Love is the acid test of Christian spirituality. If Christian conversion is authentic, we are in a process of becoming more loving. If we are not becoming more loving, something is seriously wrong.

But how do we become more loving, and what has gone wrong if we are on the Christian spiritual journey but our heart is not more and more the heart of the Father? How do we move beyond self-interest as our number one priority? How do we get from envy, criticalness or competitiveness to compassion? How do we learn to genuinely love the neighbors who are in our life and the strangers who will inevitably enter it at the worst possible moments?

LOVE AND THE CROSS

When I am confronted with my frequent failures in love, my first instinct has always been to try harder. I recognize the poverty of my love. I recall how love is the single most important criterion of my spiritual transformation. I feel regret and discouragement. I pray for help in being more loving. I try harder. And nothing changes.

The reason nothing changes is that the focus is still on me—my failures, my remorse, my discouragement, my effort. Love requires leaving all of this behind—all my self-preoccupation and all my willful striving. Love cannot be simply a result of discipline and resolve. It must flow from the heart. Regardless of the amount of love I naturally tend to have in my heart, it is not enough. The love I need is the love of God as his love becomes mine.

Christian conversion is not merely encountering love. Nor is it developing new ideas or values about love. Nor is it committing myself to trying to be loving. Christian conversion involves becoming love. But like all becoming that occurs on the Christian spiritual journey, becoming love involves death.

In spite of how central the cross is to the Christian story, Christians are always tempted to minimize its importance in their own journey. We want a spirituality of success and ascent, not a spirituality of failure and descent. We want a spirituality of improvement, not a spirituality of transformation. But the way of the cross is the way of descent, abandon and death. This is the foolishness of the gospel.

Jesus teaches us that the only truly self-fulfilled life is the life that is surrendered. Carolyn Gratton points out that "a cross comes into being when a horizontal thrust (one's human life) is interrupted by a vertical thrust (for the sake of Christ and the Gospel)."[3] Christian love emerges only from the journey through the cross. There are no short cuts that allow us to bypass the cross on the Christian spiritual journey.

The cross invites us to take the risk of losing our life so that we might truly find it (Mark 8:35). Christ teaches us that love is setting aside one's life for another. This was how he loved God. Choosing the Father's will over his own will was choosing the Father's life over his life. It was believing that his fulfillment would come not from pursuing his happiness but from pursuing God's will. Jesus believed this and he lived this. This is why we can dare trust his enigmatic and hard teaching that our own fulfillment will come only from laying down our own life for God and others.

Love and love alone is capable of making a person willing to give up his or her own life in loving others. Love always involves not just saying yes to someone but also saying no to self. The life of love is a life of death to the kingdom of self.

The conversion of the heart that lies at the core of Christian spiritual transformation begins at the cross. It involves meeting God's love in the cross, not simply encountering some judicial solution for the problem of human sin. It must also involve surrender to that love, not simply being warmed by it as a comforting spiritual truth. It must, therefore, involve genuinely experiencing God's love. For only if I have met the heart of God in love can I ever hope that his heart of love might become mine.

My own struggles to become more loving have been the most discouraging aspect of my Christian spiritual journey. But as I have begun to learn to come back through the cross to the extravagant love of God for me, slowly my hard heart is beginning to thaw. Ever so slowly my heart is becoming God's heart—larger and more tender than anything I could have ever expected or experienced as a result of my most persistent effort.

If God's heart is to become mine, I must know his heart. Meditating on God's love has done more to increase my love than decades of effort to try be more loving. Allowing myself to deeply experience his love—taking time to soak in it and allow it to infuse me—has begun to effect changes that I had given up hope of ever experiencing. Coming back to God in my failures at love, throwing myself into his arms and asking him to remind me of how much he loves me as I am—here I begin to experience new levels of love to give to others.

But again, I must come to love through the cross—come to love through sin and failure rather than success and self-improvement. It is only when I give up trying to be more loving that God's love can really touch me. It is only when I come to him in the midst of my failures in love that his love can transform me.

LOVE AS MOVEMENT FROM ME TO WE

Transformation into love is a shift from a focus on me to an aware-ness of the greater we. Fritz Kunkel developed what he called his "psychology of the we" based on this shift, which he says is the core of all genuinely Christian spiritual growth.[4]

Egocentricity and its bondage of the self is always the enemy of genuinely self-surrendering and self-transcending love. When I live with "me" as the basic reference point for life, I experience a fundamental existential alienation. Not only am I alienated from others, but paradoxically I am also alienated from my deepest self. For my deepest and truest self is not an isolated self but finds its meaning and fulfillment only in the "we" of community.

Growth in love always involves movement beyond the hard-ened boundaries of the isolated self to the selves-in-relationship that make up community. Conversion always points us toward fel-low human beings, not simply toward God. Like the grain of wheat that must fall into the earth and die if it is to flourish (John 12:24), the person who is becoming love leaves behind the broken husk of the isolated self and embraces the new possibilities of life in the human community.

Love reconnects us to life. The truth of Christ's life is that life is love and love is life. There is no genuine life without love. Self-interest suffocates life. Life implodes when self-interest is at the core. This is why the kingdom of self is based on death. Ultimately, taking care of Number One takes care of no one. For the only way to truly care for myself is to give myself in love of others. There I will find my truest and deepest fulfillment.

Love connects us to life, because the presence of genuine love always reveals the presence of God. The first letter of John tells us that "everyone who loves is begotten by God and knows God"

(1 John 4:7) and that "anyone who lives in love lives in God, and God lives in him" (4:16). "Anyone who has the Son has life, anyone who does not have the Son does not have life" (5:12).

But if love connects us to life, it offers us a life that we can no longer control. No longer can I choose whom I will love and whom I will ignore. No longer can I close my eyes to the things that hold others in bondage. For if God's heart has truly become mine, their bondage is mine. If one person suffers, all suffer (1 Corinthians 12:26). I may not always consciously experience the suffering of others. I may be reasonably successful in living the lie of autonomous existence. But my identity is based on an illusion unless it is grounded in human solidarity and community.

Transformation through love is not, therefore, as individualistic a matter as we tend to assume. When love draws me from isolation into community, your life touches mine—your pain touches me, your afflictions touch me, your anxieties touch me. In short, you become a part of me. My solidarity with you and with all human beings expands the boundaries of what I experience as my self.

In his autobiography *Long Walk to Freedom,* Nelson Mandela says that as a young man he came to understand that his freedom was inseparably tied up with that of his South African people. He found himself unable to enjoy the limited freedom he was allowed as an attorney with the privileges of education when he knew his people were not free. "Freedom is indivisible," he argues; "the chains on any one of my people were the chains on all of them, the chains on all of my people were the chains on me."[5]

Mandela has captured a profound Christian truth about the nature of love. Love that comes from the heart of God connects us to all of God's children. It also connects us to his creation—our world. God's heart of love moves me from the isolation of self-interest to a connection with life that cannot allow any ultimate divisions or categories. Love cannot exclude concern for social justice. Nor can it exclude ecological concern for the planet. Love cannot exclude concern for any human being, because all humans bear the image of the Christian God, whose heart is increasingly becoming our heart.

Alfred Adler says that the single most important criterion of psychological health is what he calls *social interest.* Social interest is a sense of solidarity with all humans. It does not allow me to limit my interest to those within my tribe—whether tribal boundaries are understood in religious, ethnic or national terms. Instead it leads to a sense of oneness with all human beings—connection with all of God's children. Nothing less than this is worthy of being called genuine love, for this is the love that flows from the heart of God.

As Angie first began to be open to God's love, she remained very isolated from other people. Apart from me, she felt quite isolated from the rest of the human race. Males she mistrusted because of her many experiences of betrayal and abuse; heterosexual women she couldn't identify with as she was a lesbian; most other lesbians she felt dismissive of because she disliked their politics; Christians she mistrusted because emotionally she related to them as if they were part of the fundamentalist past. She knew that many of these reactions were irrational. But she felt nonetheless alienated and alone.

Once again, it was her connection with God and with me that slowly began to bring the change. Gradually she began to experience a desire to reconnect with the human race. As she discovered that she had seriously misjudged both God and me, she became interested in the possibility that other people might also have a reality that was quite separate from her assumptions. Slowly she began to reach out to connect with people. First it was a gay male she thought might be emotionally safe. Then it was a small group of other spiritual seekers who were exploring reconnection to the church after a history of alienation. This group became a lifeline for her as over time they began to trust each other and together seek out a church where they might feel safe and included.

I recall a day when Angie told me a remarkable dream. She dreamed that she was the only human being on earth. At first she felt good about this, aware that she wouldn't have to share anything with anyone and wouldn't be bothered by anyone. She felt safe, she felt satisfied. But then she noticed that she was lonely. After attempting to ignore these feelings, she set out on a search for other human beings. As it began to appear that her first impressions were correct and she was the only human alive, she began to feel a deep sadness. She was overcome with a longing that she had never before known—a longing to belong.

And then she found a group of people. She was *not* alone. She was full of joy as she awoke.

Divine love did more than help Angie move beyond the pain of her past abusive experiences. And it did more than make God safe. Divine love helped her own humanity awaken. It helped her begin to move toward being love herself.

LOVE AS THE FULFILLMENT OF OUR HUMANITY

Love is the fulfillment of everything that makes us human. The ability to care deeply for others and to place their interests ahead of our own is the capstone of psychospiritual development. All psychological and spiritual problems represent, in one form or another, an impediment of love. All movement toward genuine wholeness represents growth in love.

Love aligns us with the basic design plan for the universe. Christians understand that the love of God is the most basic ingredient in the cosmos. From the beginning, God's love is the source of all that is. From the beginning love has been the way of creation, because creation is of God.

James Olthuis describes this cosmic dynamic of love as follows:

> To live is to let love well up and stream through us as the beat, pulse, and rhythm of our lives, connecting us to ourselves, our neighbors, the whole family of earth's creatures, and God, the alpha and omega of love. To love (which is to live) is to be seeking, fostering, and sustaining connections with that which is different and other—without domination, absorption, or fusion, in delight, in care, in compassion.[6]

Because God is love, and because human beings are made in God's image, love is who we are. Love is not, first and foremost, something that we do. More basically, it is who we are.

> It is in loving (or not loving) that we are (or are not) human. It is in heeding the call of love—in making life-affirming connections—that we become human. . . . Loving is not merely one thing among others that we are called to do—an extraordinary achievement, a heroic gesture that completes ordinary acts and raises them to a higher level. Love is not an additive, a spiritual supplement reserved for saints. . . . Loving is of the essence of being human, the connective tissue of reality, the oxygen of life.[7]

The point of being human is to learn love. We are more or less human insofar as we are in the school of love. As was the case for the prodigal son, the place where we learn true love is the path we take to come home to the embrace of our Creator God.

Learning love is a journey back to the reality of the First Love of our lives—the love that was there before we experienced any rejection and that will remain after all rejections. Learning love is accepting the invitation to reclaim the truth of our belovedness. Learning love is letting ourselves be loved fully and extravagantly. We learn to trust that in this love we come to the fulfillment of our humanity and the fulfillment of our calling.

There is nothing more important than learning love, because this is learning that counts for eternity. Learning to love is preparation for union with God. This was the purpose of our creation and is our destiny. Learning to love is therefore the core task of the human psychospiritual journey.

LOVE AND THE THREEFOLD CONVERSION

Alan Jones calls the learning of love the process of soul making.[8] Following the pattern of the three classic stages of Christian spiritual formation (purgation, illumination and union), he suggests that becoming truly and fully a human soul involves three stages of transformation. We could also call them three stages of conversion.

The first stage—purgation—involves awakening, encounter, the beginning of hope, and leaving everything behind to follow Jesus. It is like falling in love.

This is precisely what we see in the lives of the disciples after their first encounter with Jesus. Jesus was the One for whom they had longed, hoped and prayed. Leaving all and following him was easy. It took no thought at all. It was the expression of hearts that were bursting with joy, enthusiasm and the first blush of love.

But this first stage of conversion must be followed by a second if we are to fully become love. As we continue to follow Christ on the transformational journey, we will inevitably encounter moments in which everything begins to fall apart. Like the disciples during Christ's passion, we feel that our whole life is about to be torn from us.

This second stage has none of the warm and pleasant feelings associated with the first. It is experienced as crisis and manifested in tears, anguish and despair. At its core it involves what St. Bernard calls movement from loving God for my sake to loving him for his sake.[9] It is a hard painful conversion that is essential if we are to enter into mature love. We are led into such love by means of illumination—that is, "seeing what it might mean to love God with all our powers of mind and heart."[10] This seeing requires ripping away the self-delusions that blind us. It involves beginning to see God as he really is, not as I wish him to be. Thus it always involves a harsh confrontation with reality.

Peter's denial of Christ and subsequent deep remorse illustrate this second stage of conversion. The illumination came when he looked into Jesus' eyes and saw that he was still deeply loved. This new seeing had implications for how he saw himself as well as how he saw God. But it also matured his love for God and others. Now he knew with certainty that he was loved in the midst of his sin and failure.

Receiving God's embrace of love in the midst of my most profound awareness of my sin cannot help but propel me through self-preoccupation toward more authentic love. The love I feel for God at this point is different from that associated with the first enthusiastic burst of joy. The humbling encounter with the depths of my sin leads to a love for God that is grounded in an appreciation for grace. And any genuine encounter with grace has the effect of deepening my love of others.

But our conversion is not yet complete. The third stage of transformation into love also begins with a crisis. This crisis is precipitated not by awareness of the depths of my sin but by the seeming abandonment of God.

The third stage is illustrated by the disciples who, having followed Christ to the foot of the cross and then through it to the resurrection, are left baffled and alone as he ascends to the Father. Now he seems gone for good. But fortunately the story doesn't end there. If the ascension illustrates the crisis of this third stage, Pentecost represents its fulfillment. There the disciples discovered that they were not alone—they were, in fact, eternally united to Christ through the indwelling presence of his Spirit. In this union their love was made complete, for now the life of the Spirit was their life and the love of God was their love.

The danger of any stage theory is that it suggests a mechanical and linear movement through a process. Clearly life does not unfold in this way. A delineation of stages might also suggest work to be undertaken or tasks to be accomplished. But such work would inevitably be in the service of the ego and not genuinely transformational. Growth in love is not an accomplishment but the receipt of a gift.

However, if stages are not interpreted in an overly literal fashion they can be helpful in understanding the process of our growth in love. And if we can resist the temptation to turn them into something we do to achieve a desired end, they can help us focus on God, who is the source of any genuine transformation.

Conversion is a process—a lifelong journey of formation, deformation and re-formation. It is the ongoing journey of being born and reborn and reborn again—over and over. But rather than being bad news, suggesting a job that is never ending, this is actually good news, revealing a life than is never ending![11]

Learning to love is learning to live. It is becoming fully human. It is nothing less than the reason for our existence. In it alone do we find our deepest fulfillment. For if we find love we find God. And if we find God, we have found love.

MORE LIVES TRANSFORMED BY LOVE

Writing this chapter has again brought a number of people to my mind—not persons with naturally sunny dispositions who seemed to find love easy but those whom I have seen transformed through and into love.

I think of Mila, a young girl who had as tragic and horrific a set of childhood experiences as anyone I have ever met. A victim of malicious and prolonged abuse by her natural parents, she was removed by the state and placed in a foster home, where she was again sexually and physically abused. Years of corrective surgery were required to repair the damage to her body. The damage to her soul was, not surprisingly, even more severe.

Given that Mila experienced eight years of intense psychotherapy with me, it is tempting to think that the changes in this young woman were primarily the result of my therapeutic ministrations. I don't deny that our relationship has been tremendously important in the growth she has experienced. But I do not believe that psychotherapy could ever have been sufficient to help her know love in the intimate and prolonged ways that would be necessary to overcome abuse and actually become love.

That came from living with a Christian foster family who, almost unbelievably, managed to avoid being drawn into Mila's repeated efforts to make them reject her and treat her as she felt she deserved. Gently they communicated to her the grace that they knew in their relationship to God. Gradually they also introduced her to the source of that grace. Slowly both faith and trust began to develop. And ever so slowly she began to walk the long road toward her healing that ultimately nurtured an ability to not just receive love but give it.

Now a young woman, living independently and working in a nursery as a childcare aide, Mila has found her way back into the human community. Bright and articulate, she recently told me that love was the risk she "couldn't afford not to take." Both the giving and the receiving of love continued to be instrumental in her transformation.

What a privilege to have been part of this remarkable young woman's story. Through our work together she has taught me an enormous amount about the transforming nature of love.

I also think of a very close male friend. Years of a secret sexual addiction and great distance between a well-respected public self and a hidden private self became suddenly visible in a widely publicized crime for which he was convicted and served a number of years in prison.

Like Mila's, his transformation included a number of ingredients, but central to these was the faithful love of his wife. Although she was devastated by his betrayal, she was eventually able to forgive him and renew her love for him. Then, gently and patiently, she showed him the face of grace that has helped him become one of the most thoroughly Christian persons I have ever known. The mark of that Christian work of transformation is his love—love that reaches out through him and touches everyone he meets and the many people he spends his days supporting in intercessory prayer.

Real change is possible. We do not have to be victims of either our personality or our past. The gospel proclaims the availability of transforming love for all persons, and the process of that transformation is the same for all. Only the details of our journeys differ.

FOR FURTHER REFLECTION

But the story that can best help you reflect on the question of transformation through and into love is your own. Take some time to think about your own journey of transformation into the loving heart and character of the Christian God.

Try to be brutally honest in answering the following questions. Pretending is not the same as being. Accept no substitutes for the heart of the God who is love and who wants to make his heart ours.

- What difference does God's love of you make in your life and relationships? Is your love of others increasing? If not, consider whether you really know God's love or merely know about it.

- Is God's love moving you beyond the comfortable sphere of caring only for your own kind of people to deeply care for all people? As God's heart becomes your heart, expect that his love of the whole world (John 3:16; 1 Timothy 2:4) will become your love.

- How would you describe your own love of God? Is it growing, and is devotion increasingly your motive for obedience? Or is it limited or nonexistent? If the latter, does something in your spirit respond to God's Spirit with longing for a real love relationship with God? What steps might you want to take to respond to such a longing?

Epilogue
THE SPIRITUAL
JOURNEY

In spite of how it might sometimes appear, Christian spirituality is not a set of beliefs. Nor is it a list of prohibitions or obligations. Nor is it a spiritual self-improvement program. Christian spirituality is a journey toward union with God. First and foremost, therefore, it is a relationship.

A RELATIONSHIP WITH GOD

Christians make the seemingly preposterous claim to be able to experience a personal relationship with God. What an astounding thought, that humans can not only know God but have a personal relationship with the divine! But how easily we trivialize such a relationship if we suggest that it can develop in the first moments of conversion. Instant familiarity produces pseudo-intimacy—whether this be with God or with human beings.

Relationships that involve genuine intimacy require time and shared experience. Knowing a person, rather than simply knowing about them, demands spending time with that person. It requires listening to them, not only talking to them. And it involves simply being with them, passing time that is uncluttered by words and activities.

These same qualities of relationship hold true with God as well. Studying about God's character does not necessarily produce friendship with God. Talking to others about your ideas about God does not produce intimacy with God. There is no substitute for simply spending time with God if Christian spirituality is your journey.

Tragically, we too often spend our time working for God rather than simply being with Jesus. Like Martha, we are sure what God wants us from us is our kingdom activities and efforts. But as Martha was scurrying around serving Jesus, her sister Mary sat at his feet, gazing into his face—and Jesus said Mary had chosen the better part (Luke 10:38-42). Instead of working for God, she had learned to do God's work. What Jesus wanted was her friendship. Service would come out of this but should never replace it. The same is true for us.

SPIRITUALITY AS A JOURNEY

Describing Christian spirituality as a journey has become quite popular of late, as the journey metaphor has been increasingly applied to our life experience. But the image is not new. And applying it to Christian spirituality is firmly rooted in Scripture.

Jesus described himself as "the Way"—that is, the route to God (John 14:6). This became one of the earliest ways of referring to Christians, who were often described as being "followers of the

Way" (Acts 9:2). Journey imagery is also reflected in Christ's call of the disciples, which usually took the form of a simple invitation to follow him (for example, Matthew 4:19).

The image of journeying with Jesus highlights the relational nature of Christian spirituality. Christians are not simply commanded to go somewhere or other or do something or other. They are invited to follow Jesus—that is, travel with Jesus.

Through the Holy Spirit who dwells within me, I journey with Jesus and Jesus journeys with me. What a remarkable notion. The implication is that I share his life—a life lived two thousand years ago—as I come to know him, love him and follow him. My sufferings are, in some mysterious way, his sufferings (Romans 8:17), my holiness his (Hebrews 12:10). But equally remarkably, as I live my life as a Christ-follower, he shares my life with me. He accompanies me on my journey. And he promises to be with me always, even to the end of time (Matthew 28:20).

The journey that we take with Jesus is obviously not a journey through space but a journey through time. It is not a journey to some physical-spatial destination. It is a journey of growth and transformation. It is a journey of growing into "the fulness of Christ" (Ephesians 4:13). It is a journey of progressive union with God.

UNION AS THE GOAL

The notion of union with God is unfamiliar to some Christians, since often the destination of the journey has been described as becoming like Christ, or as acquiring the fruit of the Spirit. While these are also helpful ways of describing the journey, the ancient Christian understanding of the goal as union with God has one great advantage. It reminds us that the journey is not about achievement but about relationship.

Union is not fusion. My becoming united with Christ does not annihilate my being as a separate self. Rather, I find my truest and deepest self in Christ, and this "me-in-Christ" then becomes my new self.

Union in God is such a fundamental alignment of my being with his that it leaves the soul "like a stone that has reached the center of the earth."[1] In union with God life becomes a simple response of surrender to God's will—whatever this involves. This is because union with God involves the perfection of love. It represents the end point of transformation into love.

The Christian spiritual journey consists of more than surrender to love. But it contains nothing more important. Surrender to God's love involves confession, repentance, obedience and service. But as I have noted, for surrender to be transformational it must be surrender to love. And for it to lead to union with God, it must be surrender to *perfect love.*

Christian spirituality begins with love and ends with love. I end this book, therefore, with a prayer that I have prayed for years for my wife and son and that I regularly pray for my friends. It is my prayer for you who have followed me to this point on the journey we have shared in this book.

My prayer is my own loose rendering of that offered by Paul for the church he founded in Ephesus (Ephesians 3:16, 19):

> This, then, is what I pray for you. I ask that the Spirit of God give you the power for your spirit to grow strong and that, rooted and grounded in love, you will be able to understand the breadth and the length, the height and the depth of Christ's everlasting love for you.

Dare to pray this for yourself. Dare to believe that this is God's prayer for you. And dare to make this love yours and allow it to become the foundation of your identity.

This is union with Christ in God, the goal of the Christian spiritual journey. It will be the fulfillment of the deepest longings of your soul.

NOTES

PREFACE: SURRENDER, LOVE AND SPIRITUALITY
[1]Carl Jung, *Aspects of the Masculine* (Princeton, N.J.: Princeton University Press, 1989), p. 59.
[2]John O'Donohue, *Eternal Echoes: Celtic Reflections on Our Yearning to Belong* (New York: HarperCollins, 1999), p. xxii.

CHAPTER 1: IT ALL BEGINS WITH LOVE
[1]James H. Olthuis, *The Beautiful Risk: A New Psychology of Loving and Being Loved* (Grand Rapids, Mich.: Zondervan, 2001), p. 43.
[2]This woman's story was introduced in my book *Sacred Companions: The Gift of Spiritual Friendship and Direction* (Downers Grove, Ill.: InterVarsity Press, 2002), pp. 111-17, where I described her work with me in spiritual direction.
[3]A. W. Tozer, *The Divine Conquest* (Old Tappan, N.J.: Fleming H. Revell, 1950), p. 26.
[4]Ibid., p. 67.
[5]A. W. Tozer, *The Pursuit of God* (Camp Hill, Penn.: Christian Publications, 1982), p. 14.
[6]Ibid., p. 49.

CHAPTER 2: LOVE AND FEAR
[1]James H. Olthuis, *The Beautiful Risk: A New Psychology of Loving and Being Loved* (Grand Rapids, Mich.: Zondervan, 2001), p. 75.
[2]Søren Kierkegaard, *The Concept of Anxiety*, trans. Reidar Thomte (Princeton, N.J.: Princeton University Press, 1980).
[3]Philip Yancey, *What's So Amazing About Grace?* (Grand Rapids, Mich.: Zondervan, 1997), p. 45.

CHAPTER 3: SURRENDER AND OBEDIENCE
[1]Richard Rohr, *The Spirituality of Imperfection*, audiotape A6711 (Cincinnati, Ohio:

St. Anthony Messenger, 1997).

[2]Richard Rohr, *Everything Belongs: The Gift of Contemplative Prayer* (New York: Crossroad, 1999), pp. 121-22.

[3]Tertullian, quoted in Leonid Ouspensky, *Theology of the Icon* (New York: St. Vladimir's Press, 1978), p. 88.

[4]Francis de Sales, *The Treatise on the Love of God,* trans. Henry B. Mackey (Rockford, Ill.: Tan Books, 1997).

CHAPTER 4: TRANSFORMED BY LOVE

[1]Quoted in Trevor Hudson, *Christ Following: Ten Signposts to Spirituality* (Grand Rapids, Mich.: Fleming H. Revell, 1996), p. 67.

[2]George Benson, *The Silent Self: A Journey of Spiritual Discovery* (Cincinnati: Forward Movement, 1992), p. 84.

[3]Gerald May, *Will and Spirit: A Contemplative Psychology* (San Francisco: Harper & Row, 1983), p. 135.

[4]Hudson, *Christ Following,* p. 77.

[5]Ibid., p. 81.

CHAPTER 5: BECOMING LOVE

[1]Henri Nouwen, *The Return of the Prodigal Son* (New York: Doubleday, 1992), pp. 120-33.

[2]Ibid., p. 125.

[3]Carolyn Gratton, *The Art of Spiritual Guidance* (New York: Crossroad, 2000), p. 229.

[4]Fritz Kunkel, *Selected Writings,* ed. John A. Sanford (New York: Paulist, 1984).

[5]Nelson Mandela, *Long Walk to Freedom* (Boston: Little, Brown, 1994), p. 544.

[6]James H. Olthuis, *The Beautiful Risk: A New Psychology of Loving and Being Loved* (Grand Rapids, Mich.: Zondervan, 2001), p. 44.

[7]Ibid., p. 69.

[8]Alan Jones, *Soul Making: The Desert Way of Spirituality* (San Francisco: Harper & Row, 1985), pp. 159-84.

[9]Bernard of Clairvaux, *On Loving God,* trans. Robert Walton (Kalamazoo, Mich.: Cistercian, 1996).

[10]Jones, *Soul Making,* p. 179.

[11]Ibid., p. 168.

EPILOGUE

[1]Benedict J. Groeschel, *The Journey Toward God* (Ann Arbor, Mich.: Servant, 2000), p. 146.